THE 14TH-CENTURY ENGLISH MYSTICS

GARLAND REFERENCE LIBRARY
OF THE HUMANITIES
(VOL. 190)

CONTENTS

Library of Congress Cataloging in Publication Data

Lagorio, Valerie Marie, 1925–
    The 14th-century English mystics.

    (Garland reference library of the humanities ;
v. 190)
    Includes index.
    1. Mysticism—England—History—Bibliography.
2. Mysticism—History—Middle Ages, 600–1500—
Bibliography.   3. Mystics—England—Bibliography.
I. Bradley, Ritamary, 1916–   joint author.
II. Title.
Z7819.L33 [BV5077.G]   016.2482′2′0942   79-7922
ISBN 0-8240-9535-9   AACR1

Printed on acid-free, 250-year-life paper
Manufactured in the United States of America

THE 14TH-CENTURY ENGLISH MYSTICS

A Comprehensive Annotated Bibliography

Valerie Marie Lagorio
Ritamary Bradley

GARLAND PUBLISHING, INC. • NEW YORK & LONDON
1981

PREFACE

In compiling this bibliography, we have adopted a rather broad definition of mysticism as the progressive spiritual life, moving through purgation and illumination to union. Given our focus on the 14th-century English mystics, our definition concerns the Western Christian mystical tradition, in which union is achieved between an individual and a personal God, with accounts of the *via mystica* as diverse as the experts' attempts to assess it.

As our survey indicates, this corpus of writings has been approached from many disciplines—theology, philosophy, literature, history, psychology, sociology, and linguistics—which attest to its variety and complexity. We hope this bibliographical overview will point to many new avenues of study and research.

We have tried to gather and assess the scholarship on the mystics over the past 100 years, and have included general background information on mysticism and on the English mystics; the five major figures: Richard Rolle, the *Cloud* author, Walter Hilton, Julian of Norwich, and Margery Kempe; the secondary (in the sense of lesser-known) mystical writings, many of which are Middle English translations of Latin treatises written in England and on the Continent; and a brief assessment of the ongoing post-Reformation tradition of medieval English spirituality. In general, we have excluded book reviews, M.A. theses, the Continental mystics, and the *Imitation of Christ*, considered by many to be mystical in the *Devotio Moderna* tradition.

We would like to express our appreciation to Father Charles Heiser of the St. Mary's Divinity Library and to the staff of the Pius XII Library, St. Louis University, and to the acquisitions and research staffs of the University of Iowa Libraries for their invaluable assistance.

Valerie Marie Lagorio
Ritamary Bradley

ABBREVIATIONS

ABR	*American Benedictine Review*
AISP	*Archivio italiano per la storia della pietà*
Archiv	*Archiv für das Studium der neueren Sprachen und Literaturen*
B.L.	British Library
B.N.	Bibliothèque Nationale
C&C	*Cross and Crown*
CQR	*Church Quarterly Review*
CR	*Clergy Review*
DR	*Downside Review*
EETS	Early English Text Society
E.S.	Extra Series
O.S.	Original Series
EIC	*Essays in Criticism*
ELH	*A Journal of English Literary History*
ES	*Englische Studien*
FCEMN	*14th-Century English Mystics Newsletter*
JEGP	*Journal of English and Germanic Philology*
JEH	*Journal of Ecclesiastical History*
LQHR	*London Quarterly and Holborn Review*
LS	*Life of the Spirit*
MA	*Medium Aevum*
MLR	*Modern Language Review*
MS	*Medieval Studies*
N&Q	*Notes and Queries*
NCW	*New Catholic World*
NM	*Neuphilologische Mitteilungen*
OED	*The Oxford English Dictionary*
PMLA	*Publications of the Modern Language Association*
RES	*Review of English Studies*
SPCK	*Society for the Promotion of Christian Knowledge*
TLS	*Times Literary Supplement*
VS	*La Vie Spirituelle*

THE 14TH-CENTURY
ENGLISH MYSTICS

I. AN INTRODUCTION TO MYSTICISM AND THE ENGLISH MYSTICS

A. GENERAL WORKS ON MYSTICISM

As Aidan Cardinal Gasquet once remarked, mysticism is a word which begins with "mist" and ends with "schism." To dispel the former and avoid the latter, we have assembled the following list of books and articles which we consider to be both penetrating and responsible, as well as providing a broad background for ensuing studies of the English mystics.

1. Ahern, Barnabas. "Christian Perfection, Contemplation, and Purgatory, and the Dialogue of St. Catherine of Genoa." *American Ecclesiastical Review*, 118 (1948), 81-90.

   An in-depth examination of the relation between Christian perfection and infused contemplation--a question on which theologians and spiritual directors are divided. Ahern finds in *The Treatise on Purgatory of St. Catherine of Genoa* the answer that infused contemplation is the normal way to perfect purity of spirit.

2. Alcott, E. "What is Christian Mysticism?" *C&C*, 26 (1974), 393-403.

   Viewing Christian mysticism as "an interpersonal communion in love," Alcott recommends learning from the meditative techniques of the East, calls the mystical awakening a revolutionary experience, and foresees a revival of mystical spirituality in today's world equal to that of the 14th century.

3. Axters, Stephanus Gerard. *The Spirituality of the Low Countries*. Trans. Donald Attwater. London: Blackfriars Publications, 1954.

A learned assessment and distillation of Low Countries'
spirituality, from its early medieval origins through
Hadewych, Ruysbroeck and his followers, especially Denis
the Carthusian, and the *Devotio Moderna*. Of great interest
as background for the English mystics.

4. Baumgardt, David. *Great Western Mystics: Their Lasting
   Significance*. New York: Columbia Univ. Press, 1961.

   Originally presented as the Matchette Lecture of 1955,
   this book upholds that mystical experience can be properly
   approached by the methodology of humanistic and naturalis-
   tic philosophy. Especially recommended are "What is
   Mysticism?" and "The Mysticism of Inwardness."

5. Benz, Ernst. *Die Vision: Erfahrungsforman und Bilderwelt*.
   Stuttgart: Ernst Klett Verlag, 1969.

   An important study on visions and visionaries, of special
   interest for its treatment of Richard Rolle, Julian of
   Norwich, Catherine of Siena, and Birgitta of Sweden.

6. Bouyer, Louis. "Mysticism: An Essay on the History of a
   Word." In *Mystery and Mysticism: A Symposium*. Ed. A.
   Plé. New York: Philosophical Library, 1956, pp. 119-37.

   An overview of the field of mystical theology by a noted
   expert.

7. Bullough, Sebastian. "The Spiritual Life. An Historical
   Approach--III. The Medieval Development." *LS*, 13
   (1959), 349-57.

   Placing the great medieval mystics in an historical
   framework, Bullough explores lines of differences among
   mystics--English, Continental, and Eastern.

8. Butler, Cuthbert. *Western Mysticism*. London: Constable
   & Co., Ltd., 1922, 1924; 2nd ed. with "Afterthoughts,"
   1927, 1951; New York: E.P. Dutton and Co., 1924; 2nd ed.
   1951.

   A systematic study on mysticism from the standpoint of
   what three mystics--Saints Augustine, Gregory, and Bernard--
   thought about their experiences, as witnessed by their
   writings. "Afterthoughts" deals with "Current Controver-
   sies on Mystical Theology." The book's title denotes not
   "mysticism in the West" but "the native mysticism of the
   West that prevailed in Western Europe during the six
   centuries from St. Benedict to St. Bernard, and has charac-

teristics of its own, marking it off from later kinds and still rendering it peculiarly appropriate for Westerners."

9. Capps, Walter Holden, and Wendy Wright, eds. *Silent Fire: An Invitation to Western Mysticism.* San Francisco: Harper and Row, 1978.

   An excellent survey of Christian mysticism from Augustine to Ernesto Cardenal and Thomas Merton, with a broad contextual introduction, and with concise, informative essays introducing each selection. The work is also an excellent text or adjunct text for a course on Christian mysticism.

10. Chapman, John. "What is Mysticism?" *DR*, N.S. 27 (1928), 12-24.

    Explaining mysticism primarily in terms of knowledge, based on the discipline of philosophy, this article is intended in part for spiritual directors.

11. Clark, James M. *The Great German Mystics: Eckhart, Tauler and Suso.* Oxford: Basil Blackwell, 1949.

    A concise objective overview of 14th-century German mysticism, including not only the three main figures but also Rulman Merswin, the Friends of God, and Franciscans, with a good bibliography, consisting primarily of Continental studies. Clark offers a strong apologia for Eckhart's orthodoxy.

12. Coward, Harold, and Terence Penelhum, eds. *Mystics and Scholars.* Waterloo, Ontario: Wilfred Laurier Univ. Press, 1977.

    A report on the Calgary Conference on Mysticism, which was convened in 1976 to ponder and assess the nature of mysticism in its Eastern, Western, and North American Indian forms, and which was conducted by a dialogue between practicing mystics and scholars. Especially recommended is Walter H. Principe's "Mysticism: Its Meaning and Varieties," pp. 1-18, which surveys the best-known forms of mysticism within Eastern and Western cultures, and raises important questions for the continuing study of mysticism.

13. Dauncey, Guy. "A Report. Re-awakening Christian Mysticism." *The Teilhard Review*, 13 (1978), 104.

    Dauncey, following Fr. William Johnston, points to the Christian Church's discouragement of direct religious

experience, so that mystics like Julian of Norwich and
Teilhard are almost unknown to many people. The prospect
of inter-communication among world religions, according
to Dauncey, lies with the distinct traditions of Christian
mysticism.

14. Dawson, Christopher. "The Dark Mirror." *Dublin Review*,
    No. 375 (1939), pp. 177-200.

    Includes pertinent comments on medieval mystics.

15. Deanesly, Margaret. *The History of the Medieval Church,
    590-1500*. London: Methuen and Co., 1925.

    An important background study of "the medieval attitude
    towards life, religion and the church, of the faith and
    ideals of medieval churchmen, and the actual working of
    the medieval church system." Touches briefly on Rolle,
    Julian, and Margery Kempe, and also explores Lollardry
    and Continental heresies.

16. Denifle, Heinrich Seuse. *Die deutschen Mystiker des 14.
    Jahrhunderts*. Freiburg in der Schweiz: Paulus Verlag,
    1951.

    This is a reprint of a classic on research on Middle
    High German mysticism, written more than a century ago.
    The fame of this work rests on the assumption, quite new
    in Denifle's time, that vernacular medieval mysticism
    can only be evaluated properly if it is seen against the
    background of the tradition of Latin theology and mys-
    ticism.

17. Douglas-Smith, Basil. "The Intelligence of the Mystics."
    DR, 89 (1971), 147-52.

    Taking Poulain's definition of mysticism, "an experimen-
    tal knowledge of God's presence, analogous to sensory
    perception," the author holds that the mystics possess a
    high degree of the *intellectus* of the scholastics.

18. Dupré, Louis. "The Mystical Experience of the Self and
    Its Philosophical Significance." *Proceedings of the
    American Catholic Philosophical Association*, 48 (1974),
    149-65.

    A penetrating study of the striking differences between
    the ordinary and the mystical self, as expressed in the
    writings of the mystics.

19. Editorial. "What is Mysticism?" *LS*, 2 (1947), 49-51.

    A succinct analysis of mysticism, arriving at a defini-
    tion: "An adherence of the inmost spirit to God, through
    the will, accompanied by a profound intuition of that
    union."

20. Fairweather, William. *Among the Mystics*. Edinburgh:
    T. & T. Clark, 1936.

    A broad but balanced survey of mysticism, as defined
    by William James, entailing the rise of mysticism in the
    East and West. This work includes a brief discussion
    of pre-Reformation mysticism in England and on the
    Continent, a long section on post-Reformation Catholic
    and Protestant mystics, and an ending discussion on the
    basic principles and main features of Christian mysticism.

21. Farges, Albert. *Mystical Phenomena*. Trans. S.P.
    Jacques. London: Burns, Oates & Washbourne, 1926.

    A treatise on mystical theology, based on the principles
    of St. Teresa of Avila. Written primarily for spiritual
    directors, the work distinguishes the active, ascetic
    way from the passive, mystical way, and also deals with
    such accidental mystical phenomena as visions, ecstasy,
    and stigmatization.

22. Gardet, Louis. *La Mystique*. Paris: Presses Universi-
    taire de France, 1970.

    This work is primarily a comparison of Eastern with
    Western mystical traditions.

23. Garrigou-Lagrange, Reginald. *Christian Perfection and
    Contemplation*. Trans. Sister M. Timothea Doyle.
    London and St. Louis: B. Herder Book Co., 1937.

    A systematic study of mysticism treated as a division
    of moral theology, according to the teachings of Thomas
    Aquinas and John of the Cross. As a theologian, the
    author holds that "mystical contemplation is only the
    plenitude of the life of faith."

24. ————. *The Three Ages of the Interior Life*. Trans.
    Sister M. Timothea Doyle. 2 vols. St. Louis: B.
    Herder Book Co., 1947-8.

    A summary of the traditional systematic courses offered
    in Catholic seminaries since the 1940's on the purgative,

illuminative, amd unitive ways of growth in the spiritual
life. The author mentions Augustine Baker's *Sancta
Sophia*, Julian of Norwich, and Ruysbroeck, and identifies
"infused contemplation" with the mystical life.

25. Graef, Hilda C. "Is Mysticism Normal?" *LS*, 1 (1946),
     84-7.

     Reviewing Saudreau, Poulain, and Garrigou-Larange, the
     author replies to objections to the claim that mysticism
     is a normal part of Christian life.

26. ———. *The Light and the Rainbow*. London: Longmans,
     1959.

     Contains a substantial section on Julian, pp. 262-77.

27. ———. *The Story of Mysticism*. New York: Doubleday
     and Co., Inc., 1965.

     Written in the interests of ecumenism and catholicity,
     and based at times on modern psychology to explain the
     mystical process, this book introduces the lay reader
     to mysticism. Contents range from a brief survey of
     non-Christian mysticism, through a history of mysticism
     in the Eastern and Western Church, to the "mystical"
     14th century, to mysticism in the Reformation and Counter-
     Reformation; the book concludes with modern mystics.
     Also recommended by the same author: *The Way of the
     Mystics*. Westminster, Md.: Newman Book Co., 1948.

28. Harkness, Georgia. *Mysticism: Its Meaning and Message*.
     Nashville, Tenn.: Abingdon Press, 1973.

     A balanced study of mysticism through the ages.
     Chap. 5, "The Fertile Fourteenth Century," concentrates
     almost exclusively on the Rhineland and Flemish mystics.

29. Harper, Ralph. *Human Love, Existential and Mystical*.
     Baltimore: Johns Hopkins Press, 1966.

     "Mystical" in this book means in a broad sense the
     human person's love for God. Harper cites Julian and
     Hilton in his study of the similarities between contem-
     plative and human loves.

30. Holmes, Urban T. "Theology and Religious Renewal."
     Anglican Theological Review, 62 (1980), 3-19.

     Holmes briefly discusses such mystics as Hugh of St.
     Victor and Richard Rolle, and makes reference to William

Johnston in this analysis of American anti-intellectualism in religion. Holmes hypothesizes that theology broke from religion by the twelfth century, and since then, Christians have been suspicious of theologians, or, indeed, of any intellectual approach to religion. Holmes deplores this impasse, and suggests ways to wed theology and religion.

31. Hughes, Thomas H. *The Philosophic Basis of Mysticism*. Edinburgh: T. & T. Clark, 1937.

An examination of the epistemological, psychological, and ethical aspects of the mystical life.

32. Inge, William R. *Mysticism in Religion*. Chicago: Univ. of Chicago Press, 1948.

In one of his last books treating mysticism, Inge includes a chapter on "Some Medieval and English Mystics," in order "to direct my readers to some of the most attractive and beautiful mystical books in our language." A standard work on mysticism, although not all will share Inge's views.

33. ————. *The Awakening of the Soul. An Introduction to Christian Mysticism*. London: A.R. Mowbray & Co., 1959.

Taking mysticism as "communion with God," Dean Inge urges the practice of prayer.

34. James, William. *The Varieties of Religious Experience*. Gifford Lectures on Natural Religion Delivered at Edinburgh in 1901-2. New York: Modern Library, 1929.

This classic study of religious experience treats explicitly of mysticism in Lectures 16 and 17, and touches incidentally on the subject throughout the work. The lectures have long been considered a standard work on the psychology of the religious impulse. James takes the position that the mystical tradition is little altered by "differences of clime and creed," a view with which many theologians and mystics disagree.

35. Johnston, William. *The Still Point. Reflections on Zen and Christian Mysticism*. New York: Harper and Row, 1971.

Johnston explores points of contact between Zen Buddhist insight and Christian contemplation, with citations from

The Cloud of Unknowing. An excellent popular approach
to the subject.

36. ————. *Silent Music: The Science of Meditation.* New
York: Harper and Row, 1974.

Some attention is given in this work to the major
figures in medieval English mysticism. The author believes that Eastern mysticism can learn "respect for
rationality" from the West.

37. ————. *The Inner Eye of Love.* New York: Harper and
Row, 1978.

An exploration of Western Christian mysticism, with an
attempt to bridge the gap between Western and Eastern
asceticism and mysticism.

38. Jones, Rufus M. *Studies in Mystical Religion.* London:
Macmillan & Co., Ltd., 1909.

Stressing the nature and value of first-hand experience in religion, Jones presents a survey of Christian
mysticism from a review of primitive Christianity through
Francis of Assisi, the Continental and especially the
German mystical movements, and post-Reformation sects.
Only in Chap. 15 is he concerned with pre-Reformation
mysticism in England, encompassing primarily Wyclif, but
also touching on Rolle, the *Cloud* author, and Hilton.

39. ————. *The Flowering of Mysticism.* New York: Macmillan
Co., 1939.

Predominantly a study of the Friends of God, with
their religion of direct illumination, in the 14th century. Chap. 12 concerns the flowering of mysticism in
England.

40. Katsaros, Thomas, and Nathaniel Kaplan. *The Western
Mystical Tradition. An Intellectual History of Western
Civilization.* Vol. I. New Haven: Yale Univ. Press,
1969.

This highly condensed history is useful for the general
reader in locating the place of the mystics and mystical
movements within the framework of the history of culture
and ideas. However, the work is marred by over-simplifi-
cation and over-generalization. Statements on mysticism
need to be reassessed: for example, it is said that
anchorites exerted no lasting influence (Julian of Norwich

is not mentioned); and there is much reliance on earlier
and inadequate judgments on such movements as that of
German mysticism in the 12th and 13th centuries. The
value of the work is that it takes mysticism seriously
as a component in the intellectual history of the West,
up to the Renaissance. It also affords an extensive
bibliography.

40a. Katz, S., ed. *Mysticism and Philosophical Analysis*.
London: Sheldon Press, 1978.

Ten essays devoted entirely to the philosophical
analysis of mysticism, covering such topics as the
nature of the mystical experience, and linguistic
inadequacy and the ineffability of the mystical experience.

41. Kelley, Placid. "Poverty and the Rhineland Mystics."
DR, 74 (1955-6), 48-66.

A competent article on the metaphysics of the Rhineland
mystics, showing that the ground of their teaching on
poverty of spirit is Eckhart's objective metaphysics
of *esse*. It clarifies much of what is often misunder-
stood in the language of the Rhineland school.

42. Knowles, David. *The Nature of Mysticism*. New York:
Hawthorn Books, Inc., 1966.

A scholarly and theological excursus on mysticism in
Catholic and other world religions, as well as nature
mysticism.

43. Leclercq, Jean. "Modern Psychology and the Interpretation of Medieval Texts." *Speculum*, 48 (1973), 476-90.

Leclercq cautions against treating a text, which may
be only literary fiction, solely from the aspect of
pathological experience. He finds that psychology has
helped by (1) suggesting questions which might not other-
wise have been raised; and (2) allowing us to trace
motivations and to approach an understanding of certain
aspects of historical situations. His views serve as a
helpful guide for the reading of mystical texts.

44. Leff, Gordon. *The Dissolution of the Medieval Outlook*.
New York: New York Univ. Press, 1976.

Chap. 4, "The Spiritual World," presents an overview
of the cry for spiritual renewal in the 14th and early

15th centuries, characterized by the rise of Christian
mysticism: the individual sought union with God within
the soul, and the institution was shaped by a Scripture-
centered call for a return to apostolic first principles
through reformation of the Church and monasticism. This
chapter concentrates on Rhineland mysticism, especially
Eckhart and his followers, with a brief mention of the
English group.

45. Lucia of the Incarnation. "The Western Spiritual Tradi-
    tion." *Way*, Suppl. 16 (1972), pp. 15-23.

    A discussion of women's continuing contribution to the
    Western spiritual tradition, citing Hildegard of Bingen,
    Mechthild of Magdeburg, Mechthild of Hackeborn, St.
    Gertrude the Great, Julian of Norwich, and Catherine of
    Siena, among others.

46. Maisonneuve, Roland. "L'Univers théologique du langage
    visionnaire." *Foi et Langage*, 9 (1979), 275-91; "Le
    Langage visionnaire chrétien." *Foi et Langage*, 13
    (1980), 45-62.

    Perceptive companion studies on the language of the
    mystics, drawing from a wide spectrum of medieval and
    modern mystics.

47. Maréchal, Joseph. *Studies in the Psychology of the
    Mystics*. Trans. Algar Thorold. London: Burns, Oates
    & Washbourne, Ltd., 1927.

    This early work, which still has valuable insights,
    attempts to treat mysticism from the viewpoints of both
    theology and psychology. Medieval English mystics are
    not considered.

48. Maxwell, Lynda. "Mystical Consciousness and the Dying."
    Contemplative Review, 10 (1977), 9-21.

    Includes citations from medieval mystics in a collec-
    tion of examples of mystical states.

49. Merton, Thomas. "The Contemplative Life, Its Meaning
    and Necessity." *Dublin Review*, 223 (1949), 26-35.

    Defines contemplation, which is not weird, esoteric,
    anti-social, or anti-intellectual, and argues for its
    necessity in the modern world.

50. Moltmann, Jürgen. "Theology of Mystical Experience."
    Scottish Journal of Theology, 32 (1979), 501-20.

A discussion of the Christocentricity of the Christian spiritual life and mystical experience.

51. Newell, William L. "Zaehner Vs. the Unity of Religions." *Ecumenist*, 16 (1968), 41-5.

This overview of the work of Robert Zaehner states that his thesis throughout was that "religious experiences and the religions that mediate them" are vastly different. Not to recognize the differences in forms of mysticism and religion is to risk losing a grip on reality. Monastic and theistic bases for mysticism are distinguished in representative accounts of religious experience. This is a useful guide, although it is focussed on 20th-century writers.

52. Otto, Rudolph. *Mysticism East and West. A Comparative Analysis of the Nature of Mysticism*. 2nd ed. New York: Meridian Books, 1957.

Meister Eckhart is the principal example of Christian mysticism discussed in this work. The book is a broad effort at synthesis, which may occasion some reservations from those who believe that the East-West dialogue must progress slowly and thoroughly.

53. ————. *The Idea of the Holy*. Trans. John W. Harvey. 2nd ed. New York: Oxford Univ. Press, 1958.

Traces the sense of the "wholly-other," showing that religion was present in human consciousness very early. Only slowly was the experience adequately translated into expression. The Judaic faith, culminating in Christianity, most perfectly translates and moralizes this numinous experience. An accepted classic of religious philosophy.

54. Parente, Pascal P. *The Mystical Life*. St. Louis: B. Herder Book Co., 1946.

This survey of traditional Catholic teachings in descriptive and speculative mystical theology also evaluates extraordinary states and phenomena. There is a useful bibliography on mystery cults and sources, texts, and studies in Christian mysticism.

55. Parrinder, Geoffrey. *Mysticism in the World's Religions*. New York: Oxford University Press, 1976.

This book's purpose is "to introduce the great religions in their mystical expressions" and to provide "clues to the diverse forms and expressions of mysticism, by con-

sidering some of the major religious traditions of East
and West."

56. Pepler, Conrad. "The Unity of Mystical Experience."
     Blackfriars, 31 (1950), 204-19.

     Opposing Aldous Huxley and Gerald Heard, the author
     reasons that if there is a unity in mysticism, it is a
     unity in Christ. Cites Walter Hilton.

57. ————. "Psychologies of Mysticism." *Dominican Studies*,
     4 (1951), 133-52.

     Defining mysticism as a description of the normal way
     of a Christian from his first infusion of grace until the
     perfect fulfillment of the beatific vision, and psychology
     as the study of the soul from a particular point of view,
     Pepler treats the four psychologies of Christian mysticism
     --empirical, general theological, "divine image" (the soul
     as the image of God), and sacramental (the soul as subject
     or recipient of sacramental activity), and concludes with
     a suggested synthesis.

58. Poulain, Augustin F. *The Graces of Interior Prayer:
     A Treatise on Mystical Theology*. Trans. Leonard L.
     Yorke Smith. London: Routledge and Kegan Paul, 1951.

     This classical treatise on the life of prayer has been
     revised to accord with the 10th French edition by J.V.
     Vainvel.

59. Pourrat, Pierre. *Christian Spirituality in the Middle
     Ages*. Trans. S.P. Jacques. Vol. II. Westminster,
     Md.: Newman Press, 1953.

     A scholarly assessment of the spirituality of the
     Benedictines, Canons Regular of St. Augustine, Francis-
     cans, and Dominicans, as these orders partake in the
     three-fold conception of spiritual science: practical
     and affective spirituality, speculative spirituality,
     and a combination, which includes both sentiment and
     reason.

60. Russell, Bertrand. *Mysticism and Logic*. Garden City,
     N.Y.: Doubleday and Co., Inc., 1957.

     Only the first chapter deals with mysticism, which
     Russell believes is built on emotion and thus is inferior
     to science. Yet he calls the emotion "the inspirer of
     whatever is best in Man."

61. Schmidt, Margot. *Rudolph von Biberach's Die siben strassen zu got.* Quaracchi-Florentiae: Typographia Collegii S. Bonaventurae, 1969.

   This thorough, scholarly work gives invaluable information on the Latin theological backgrounds of 14th-century mysticism.

62. Seesholtz, Anna G. *Friends of God. Practical Mystics of the Fourteenth Century.* New York: Columbia Univ. Press, 1934.

   This study of the milieu and leading figures of the Friends of God movement, with attention to Eckhart, Tauler, Suso, Rulman Merswin, and Ruysbroeck, concludes with the lasting influence of God's Friends.

63. Sitwell, Gerard. *Spiritual Writers of the Middle Ages.* New York: Hawthorn Books, 1961.

   A useful overview, including a chapter on "The Mystical Movement of the Fourteenth-Century." The focus is on schools of spirituality and trends in theology and philosophy as they seem to influence "that branch of Christian theology which deals with man's relation to God in all its aspects."

64. Smart, Ninian. "Interpretation and Mystical Experience." *Religious Studies,* 1 (1965), 75-87.

   Smart argues that there is not necessarily a "perennial philosophy" common to the mystics, despite the apparent sameness of mysticism in different cultures and religions.

65. Smith, Margaret. *An Introduction to the History of Mysticism.* London: SPCK, 1930; rpt. Amsterdam: Philo Press, 1970.

   Surveys mysticism in the Old and New Testaments, classical times, the early Christian Church, the Middle Ages, and modern times, as well as in the Orient. Special chapters deal with mysticism in England, Italy, and Spain, along with German and Flemish mysticism. Brief mention is made of Rolle, the *Cloud* author, Hilton, Julian, and Margery Kempe.

66. Stace, Walter T. *Mysticism and Philosophy.* New York: Macmillan Co., 1960.

   A classical introduction to mysticism through the disciplines of logic and systematic philosophy. Stace

assumes a basic unity in theistic and nontheistic mysticism, using frequent citations from Eckhart, Suso, and
Ruysbroeck. The chapter on "Mysticism and Language" is
especially useful for all mystical traditions.

67. Steere, Douglas V. "The Meaning of Mysticism Within
    Christianity." *Religion in Life*, 22 (1953), 515-26.

    A penetrating study of the significance of mystical
    experience to the Christian religion, as well as a
    consideration of the relation between mystical experience,
    especially in its supra-noetic character, and ordinary
    processes of sensory perception and discursive thought.

68. Steuart, R.H.J. "Who Are the Mystics?" *Pax*, 19 (1930),
    264-8.

    An important article which clearly defines the contem-
    plative vocation.

69. Studzinski, Raymond. "Freeing the Spirit--Toward a
    Holistic Spirituality." *Contemplative Review*, 12 (1979),
    1-10.

    This article argues that "spirituality must be con-
    cerned with the whole person as he interacts with his
    world and with the rest of humanity"; that contemporary
    asceticism must be characterized by discipline and sim-
    plicity; and that the present-day turning toward prayer
    and the returning to the writings of the great medieval
    mystics clearly indicate the parallel between the 14th
    century and our own.

70. Sylvia Mary, Sr. "Contemplation and Mysticism." *CQR*,
    164 (1963), 83-93.

    The author follows David Knowles rather than Cuthbert
    Butler in the belief that truly mystical experience is
    not the ordinary way of the Christian life.

71. Tanqueray, Adolphe. *The Spiritual Life. A Treatise on
    Ascetical and Mystical Theology*. Trans. Herman Branderis.
    Tournai: Desclée and Co., 1930.

    For many years a widely used text in Catholic seminaries
    and monasteries, this book presents the mystical life in
    a systematic form, drawing principally from Thomas
    Aquinas, and treating mysticism as scientific knowledge
    within theology. It has had great influence in forming
    Catholic opinion on the mystical life, and has sometimes

stood in the way of the direct reading of the testimony
of the mystics themselves. Notes in the bibliography
have been superseded by recent research and scholarship.

72. Tart, Charles T., ed. *Transpersonal Psychologies.*
London: Routledge and Kegan Paul; and New York: Harper
and Row, 1975.

A series of essays collected to bridge the gap between
the scientific and spiritual modes of understanding,
which helps to "revivify the too often dead theological
formulae which frequently obscure the live experience
they were formed to shape." Of special interest is
W. McNamara's "Psychology and the Christian Mystical
Tradition."

73. Underhill, Evelyn. *Mysticism. A Study in the Nature and
Development of Man's Spiritual Consciousness.* London,
1911; rpt. New York: E.P. Dutton and Co., Inc., 1961.

Many citations from the English mystics enrich this
fundamental work on the common qualities of mystical experience. The Appendix is an "Historical Sketch of
European Mysticism from the Beginning to the Christian
Era to the Death of Blake." The bibliography, though
somewhat outdated, is still valid.

74. ————. *The Mystics of the Church.* London, 1925; rpt.
New York: Schocken Books, 1964.

A consideration of the mystics in their relation to
the Church, defining a mystic as "the great creative
soul whose special experience of God does something for
his fellow-Christians, who deepens the corporate spiritual
consciousness, brings in fresh news about eternal life."
Mysticism of this sort has ever been essential to
Christianity, the author maintains. Also recommended
are the following titles by this same author: *The Mystic
Way,* 1913; *Practical Mysticism,* 1915; *The Essentials of
Mysticism,* 1920; and *Mixed Pasture,* 1933.

75. van der Leew, G. *Religion in Essence and Manifestation.*
Trans. J.E. Turner. 2nd ed. London: George Allen &
Unwin, Ltd., 1964.

Chap. 75 is devoted to mysticism.

76. Vernet, Félix. *Medieval Spirituality.* Trans. Benedictines
of Talacre. London: Sands & Co.; and St. Louis: B.

Herder Book Co., 1930.

An informative handbook, stressing the role of Benedictinism.

77. Von Hügel, Friedrich. *The Mystical Element of Religion.*
    2 vols. London, 1909; rpt. London: J.M. Dent and Sons,
    Ltd., 1961.

    A study of the philosophy of mysticism, illustrated by
    the life of Catherine of Genoa (1447-1510), with scattered
    references drawn from Julian, Roysbroeck, and Suso. The
    second volume is more general in scope. This great
    classic work stresses that the mystical element in reli-
    gion, to remain balanced, must be tempered by institu-
    tional and historical elements.

78. Watkin, Edward I. *The Philosophy of Mysticism.* London:
    Grant Richards, Ltd., 1920.

    A study of the metaphysics implicit in mystical ex-
    perience, along with an analysis of the *via mystica,*
    using St. John of the Cross as a guide.

79. ———. "Mysticism Natural and Supernatural." *Month,*
    N.S. 18 (1957), 274-81.

    Watkin disagrees with R.C. Zaehner on points of lan-
    guage, consistency of theological statements, and the
    difference between "transmutation into the divine essence"
    and transformation into God. Cites *Epistle of Privy
    Counsel.*

79a. Woods, Richard, ed. *Understanding Mysticism.* Garden
    City, N.Y.: Doubleday & Co., Inc., 1980.

    A comprehensive collection of 36 critical studies,
    covering the following disciplines: history of religions,
    phenomenology, psychology, literary criticism, sociology,
    theology, and philosophy.

80. Zaehner, Robert C. *Mysticism Sacred and Profane.* Oxford:
    Clarendon Press, 1957.

    An inquiry into comparative mysticism, exploring some
    varieties of preternatural experience, with the basic
    premise that mysticism is not essentially the same in
    all cultures. Mysticisms of the Indies, Muslim, and
    Christian religions are assessed to show similarities and
    differences, with one of the irreconcilable differences
    being monism vs. theism.

B. REFERENCE WORKS

The following are basic reference texts.
The list and its resources are not exhaustive,
but will serve as reliable guides.

81. Bowman, Mary Ann. *Western Mysticism: A Guide to the
    Basic Works.* Chicago: American Library Association,
    1978.

    A basic bibliography intended to provide a selective
    working corpus for librarians, undergraduates, and the
    general public, with categories covering the philosophy,
    history, practice, and experience of mysticism, mystical
    experience in literature, and mystical and contemplative
    writings from the patristic era to modern times. Annota-
    tions, where present, are brief.

82. *The Cambridge History of English Literature.* Eds. A.W.
    Ward and A.R. Waller. Vol. II. The End of the Middle
    Ages. New York: Macmillan Co., 1933.

    Chap. 2, "Religious Movements in the Fourteenth Century"
    by J.P. Whitney, includes Rolle, but needs assessment in
    light of later scholarship. This caution also applies to
    Chap. 12, "English Prose in the Fifteenth Century" by
    Alice D. Greenwood, which treats of Hilton and Julian.

83. *Dictionary of National Biography:* Walter Hilton, Vol. 9,
    pp. 886-7; Julian of Norwich, Vol. 10, p. 1114; Margery
    Kempe, Vol. 10, pp. 1282-3; Richard Rolle, Vol. 17,
    pp. 164-6.

84. *Dictionnaire de spiritualité ascétique et mystique doctrine
    et histoire.* Eds. Marcel Viller et al. 10 vols. 1937-
    79.

    An ongoing publication with excellent entries on the
    mystics. Of special interest are: "Anglaise ... (Spiri-
    tualité)," Félix Vernet; "Baker (David Augustin)," Justin
    McCann; "Benoit de Canfeld," M. Viller; "Denys l'Aréopa-
    gite (Le Pseudo)," J. Lécuyer et al.; "Expérience spiri-
    tuelle," Augustin Leonard; "Frères du Libre Esprit,"
    Romana Guarnieri; "Guillaume Flete," M. Benedict Hackett;
    "Hilton (Walter)," M. David Knowles and Joy Russell Smith;
    "Julienne de Norwich," Edmund Colledge and James Walsh;
    "Kempe (Margery)," M. David Knowles; "Richard Methley,
    chartreux," James Hogg.

85. Doyle, A.I. "A Survey of the Origins and Circulation of
     Theological Writings in English in the 14th, 15th, and
     Early 16th Centuries with Special Consideration of the
     Part of the Clergy Therein." Diss. 2301-2. Cambridge
     Univ. 1953.

     Of paramount importance for information about manu-
     scripts and dissemination of the mystics' writings.

86. *Encyclopedia of Religion and Ethics.* Ed. James Hastings.
     New York: Charles Scribner's Sons, 1910-34.

     Of special interest: "Mysticism, Introductory," Rufus
     M. Jones; "Mysticism (Christian, NT)," Rufus M. Jones;
     "Mysticism (Christian, Roman Catholic)," J. Chapman;
     "Mysticism (Christian, Protestant)," Rufus M. Jones.

87. Ferguson, John. *An Illustrated Encyclopedia of Mysticism
     and the Mystery Religions.* London: Thames and Hudson,
     1976.

     A concise accumulation of factual material about Eastern
     and especially Western mysticism pertinent to such fields
     of study as literature, philosophy, theology, mythology,
     and history of ideas. Useful to a wide audience.

88. *14th-Century English Mystics Newsletter.* Eds. Ritamary
     Bradley and Valerie Lagorio. University of Iowa,
     1975- .

     Concentrates on current scholarship and research-in-
     progress on the medieval mystics.

89. Hackett, David G. *The Christian-Buddhist Encounter: A
     Select Bibliography.* Berkeley: Graduate Theological
     Union Library, 1979.

     In cognizance of the increasing Buddhist/Christian
     dialogue, this annotated bibliography encompasses ap-
     proaches to dialogue, content of the dialogue, Buddhism
     and the American religious heritage, and related issues.

90. Jolliffe, Peter S. *A Check-List of Middle English Prose
     Writings of Spiritual Guidance.* Toronto: Pontifical
     Institute of Mediaeval Studies, 1974.

     A major research tool for medieval scholars, given its
     professed purpose of indicating "fruitful methods of
     approach and promising topics for further study," in an
     area of medieval English literature hitherto neglected.
     The list is limited to prose works of pastoral intention

concerned with confession and spiritual guidance, written
during the 14th and 15th centuries, and, further, is
confined to manuscripts in public and semi-public
libraries in Great Britain and Ireland.

91. *Lexikon für Theologie und Kirche*. Freiburg im Breisgau:
    Verlag Herder, 1957: "*Cloud* Author," Vol. 2, p. 1237;
    "Julian of Norwich," Vol. 5, p. 1202; "English Mysticism,"
    Vol. 7, p. 738; "Richard Rolle," Vol. 8, pp. 1292-3;
    "Walter Hilton," Vol. 10, p. 948.

92. *New Catholic Encyclopedia*. Washington, D.C.: Catholic
    University of America, 1967.

    Of special interest: "Bridget of Sweden, St.," M.S.
    Conlan; "Hilton, Walter," J. Walsh; "Julian of Norwich,"
    J. Walsh; "Mysticism," T. Corbishley; "Mysticism in
    Literature," H.C. Gardiner and E.E. Larkin; "Mystics,
    English," E. Colledge; "Rolle de Hampole, Richard," E.
    Colledge; and "Ruysbroeck, Jan Van, Bl.," E. Colledge.

93. *Oxford Dictionary of the Christian Church*. London, 1974:
    Cloud author, pp. 306-7; Walter Hilton, pp. 650-1;
    Julian of Norwich, pp. 766-7; Margery Kempe, pp. 775-6;
    Richard Rolle, pp. 1193-4.

94. *Patrologia Cursus Completus: Series Latina*. Ed. Jacques
    Paul Migne. Paris: Petit Montrange, 1844-65.

95. Phillips, Paschal. *Bibliography on Western Mysticism*.
    Conference of Major Superiors of Men Information, No.
    35. Washington, D.C.: March 17, 1977.

    A rudimentary but useful bibliography, intended for
    public libraries and the general readership section of
    college and university libraries.

96. Revell, Peter. *Fifteenth Century English Prayers and
    Meditations: A Descriptive List of Manuscripts in the
    British Library*. Garland Reference Library of the
    Humanities. New York and London: Garland Publishing,
    Inc., 1975.

    This bibliography, limited primarily to manuscripts in
    the British Library written in the 15th century, has two
    main areas of interest: Church interest of the period
    and Middle English literature. It serves as a guide to
    minor and often overlooked texts.

97. Sawyer, Michael E. *A Bibliographic Index of Five English
    Mystics*. Pittsburgh: The Clifford E. Barbour Library,

Pittsburgh Theological Seminary, 1978.

Included are Rolle, Julian, the *Cloud* author, Hilton, and Margery Kempe, with each section covering editions, modern studies, book reviews, and pertinent Master's theses and doctoral dissertations.

98. Wainwright, William J. *Philosophy of Religion: An Annotated Bibliography of Twentieth-Century Writings in English.* Garland Reference Library of the Humanities. New York and London: Garland Publishing, Inc., 1978.

     1335 items are grouped under eight principal headings, one of which concerns "Mysticism and Religious Experience." The entire work is a significant contribution to philosophical reflection on religion and God.

99. Wells, John Edwin, et al. *A Manual of the Writings in Middle English, 1050-1400.* New Haven: Yale Univ. Press, 1916, 1923-51.

     See Chap. 9, "Rolle and His Followers."

C. ANTHOLOGIES

The major avenue for the diffusion of the mystics' writings is a supply of adequate texts, both critical editions and modern English translations of individual works, published separately or in anthologies. A number of excellent anthologies have recently appeared, but several of the classic anthologies, such as Carl Horstmann's *Yorkshire Writers: Richard Rolle of Hampole* and Clare Kirchberger's *Coasts of the Country*, are very difficult to obtain. Fortunately, some are being reprinted, and it is hoped that others will be, as well.

100. Benson, Robert H. *A Book of the Love of Jesus.* London: Sir Isaac Pitman & Sons, Ltd., 1909.

     Written in modern English for devotional purposes, this work contains some Rolle meditations and lyrics, as well as *The Abbey of the Holy Ghost* (pp. 183-202), and other short works and verses.

101. Colledge, E., ed. and trans. *The Medieval Mystics of England.* New York: Charles Scribner's Sons, 1961.

Excerpts from Aelred of Rievaulx's *Mirror of Love*;
Edmund Rich's *Mirror of Holy Church*; Rolle's *Ego Dormio*;
the *Cloud* author's *Book of Privy Counsel*; Hilton's *Scale
of Perfection*; Julian's *Revelations*; and Margery Kempe's
Book, with an informative introduction on precursors
and leading figures of English mysticism.

102. ———, trans. *Mediaeval Netherlands Religious Literature*. London: London House & Maxwell, 1965.

Translations of writings of Beatrice of Nazareth,
Hadewijch of Antwerp, Mary of Nijmeghen, and Ruysbroeck
(*Book of the Sparkling Stone*), with an introduction and
bibliography.

103. De Jaegher, Paul, ed. *An Anthology of Christian Mysti-
cism*. Trans. Donald Attwater. Westminster, Md.:
Newman Press, 1950; rpt. Springfield, Ill.: Templegate
Publishers, 1977.

De Jaegher's introduction delineates the benefits that
accrue from reading the mystics, and recommends them "to
all who want to make spiritual progress." The anthology
includes a wide selection of medieval and more modern
mystical texts with an introductory note on each author.

104. Fleming, David A., ed. *The Fire and the Cloud: An
Anthology of Catholic Spirituality*. New York, Toronto,
and Ramsey, N.J.: Paulist Press, 1978.

This anthology of excerpts from primary sources,
ranging from the Fathers of the Church to Thomas Merton,
is written for the general reader.

105. Gardner, Edmund G., ed. *The Cell of Self-Knowledge*.
New York: Duffield and Co.; and London: Chatto and
Windus, 1910; rpt. New York: Cooper Square Publishers,
Inc., 1966.

A collection of the following mystical treatises, with
an introduction and notes: *Benjamin Minor* of Richard of
St. Victor; *Divers Doctrines* from the Life of Saint
Catherine of Siena; a selection from Margery Kempe's
Book; Hilton's *Of Angels' Song*; *Epistle of Prayer*;
Epistle of Discretion in Stirrings of the Soul; and *A
Devout Treatise of Discernment of Spirits*.

106. Happold, F.C. *Mysticism: A Study and an Anthology*.
Harmondsworth, Middlesex: Penguin Books, 1963.

Taking mysticism as a special type of spirituality to

be examined as "a type of experience, as a way of knowledge, and as a state of consciousness," Happold presents
a survey of mysticism, with selected writings drawn
primarily from Christian mystics.

107. Horstmann, Carl, ed. *Yorkshire Writers: Richard Rolle
      of Hampole, an English Father of the Church, and His
      Followers.* 2 vols. London: Swan Sonnenschein & Co.;
      New York: Macmillan and Co., 1895-6; rpt. Cambridge:
      D.S. Brewer, Ltd., 1978.

      An important collection of editions of Middle English
      texts of Rolle and other mystics. Selections from this
      text will be indicated throughout this bibliography by
      "H., volume number, and page."

108. Kirchberger, Clare, ed. *The Coasts of the Country: An
      Anthology of Prayer Drawn from the Early English
      Spiritual Writers.* London: Harvill Press; Chicago:
      Regnery, 1952.

      This anthology of devotional and mystical texts is
      arranged to show "the natural development of the life of
      prayer and the Spirit toward God and man, active and
      passive, from its earlier childlike beginnings to the
      more rare supernatural experience." There are notes on
      manuscripts and texts, a glossary, and a bibliography
      of manuscripts and printed editions.

109. O'Brien, Elmer, ed. *Varieties of Mystical Experience.*
      New York: New American Library, 1965.

      An anthology and interpretation of writings of major
      mystics, including Eckhart, Tauler, Suso, Ruysbroeck,
      the *Cloud* author, Hilton, and Julian, among others.

110. Petry, Ray C., ed. *Late Medieval Mysticism.* Library of
      Christian Classics, Vol. 13. Philadelphia: Westminster
      Press, 1957.

      This collection of mystical writings from Bernard to
      Catherine of Genoa stresses the Continental mystics.
      In addition to a general introduction, there are in-
      formative prefaces for each figure.

111. Renaudin, Paul. *Mystiques anglais: Richard Rolle,
      Juliane de Norwich, Le Nuage de l'inconnaissance,
      Walter Hilton.* Paris: Aubier, 1957.

      Introduction, with selected texts in French translation.

112. Stace, Walter T., ed. *The Teachings of the Mystics.*
     New York: New American Library, 1960.

     An anthology with commentary.

113. Way, Robert E. *The Wisdom of the English Mystics.* Lon-
     don: Sheldon Press, 1978.

     This work by the author of *The Garden of the Beloved*
     has an introductory survey of the English mystics, fol-
     lowed by short selections from their writings. Extends
     to the modern period.

D. FORERUNNERS OF THE ENGLISH MYSTICS

     Because the English mystics participated in
     the continuum of the Christian mystical tradi-
     tion, we recommend the following works by or
     studies concerning patristic and medieval
     writers who have, by scholarly consensus, had
     an informing influence on the 14th-century
     mystics.

114. Allen, Hope Emily. "Some Fourteenth-Century Borrowings
     from *Ancrene Riwle*." *MLR*, 18 (1923), 1-8.

     Cites evidence of borrowings from *Ancrene Riwle* in *The
     Chastising of God's Children, Poor Caitiff, Gratia Dei,*
     Rolle's *English Psalter*, and a Latin fragment of the
     early 15th century, which evince the popularity of the
     Riwle in the 14th century, two centuries after Allen
     believes it was written.

115. Anselm, St. *The Devotions of St. Anselm.* Ed. Clement
     C. Webb. London: Methuen & Co., 1903.

     An introduction to Anselm's life and works, together
     with a translation of the *Proslogion* and a series of
     meditations and prayers.

116. ———. *Prayers and Meditations of St. Anselm.* Trans.
     Benedicta Ward. Harmondsworth, Middlesex: Penguin
     Books, 1973.

     A modern English translation of the *Proslogion* and
     all the prayers and meditations.

117. Armstrong, A.H. "Platonic Mysticism." *Dublin Review*,
      216 (1945), 130-45.

      Explores what Armstrong sees as a close affinity of
      Plotinus with mystics of the Western tradition, and
      discusses Plotinian influence apart from the intellectual
      contemplation of the Platonists.

118. A Benedictine of Stanbrook. *Medieval Mystical Tradition
      and St. John of the Cross*. London: Burns and Oates,
      1954.

      An informative and clear discussion of the writings
      of Hugh and Richard of St. Victor, Bonaventure, James
      of Milan (*Stimulus Amoris*), and Hugh of Balma (*De
      Triplici Via*), in Chaps. 2-4.

119. Bernard, Charles A. "Les Formes de la théologie chez
      Denys l'Aréopagite." *Gregorianum*, 59 (1978), 39-64.

      Maintaining that Dionysius is proposing varied ap-
      proaches to God, Bernard carefully explores the apophatic
      basis of Dionysius' *Mystical Theology*, its fusion with
      the discursive theology of the *Divine Names*, and the
      comparatively neglected approach, essentially contem-
      plative, of his symbolic theology.

120. Bonaventure, St. *The Mind's Road to God*. Trans. George
      Boas. Indianapolis and New York: Bobbs-Merrill Co.,
      Inc., 1953.

      A modern English translation with introduction on
      Bonaventure's sources and on Franciscan philosophy.

121. ————. *The Soul's Journey into God. The Tree of Life.
      The Life of St. Francis*. Trans. with introduction by
      Ewart Cousins. New York, Toronto, and Ramsey, N.J.:
      Paulist Press, 1978.

      A clear and felicitous translation of these seminal
      mystical treatises, with an excellent introduction.

122. Brooke, Odo. "Faith and Mystical Experience in William
      of St. Thierry." *DR*, 82 (1964), 93-102.

      Although William's theology presents an intrinsic
      relationship between faith and mystical experience,
      Brooke feels unable to say if the intuitive aspect of
      faith in the judgment of connaturality is a sufficient
      metaphysical basis for what William means by intuition.

123. Cabussut, André. "La Dévotion au Nom de Jésus dans
     l'église d'occident." *VS*, 86 (1952), 46-69.

     An historical survey of devotion to the name of Jesus
     from the patristic age onward, centering on Anselm,
     Bernard, Francis of Assisi, and Bonaventure, among others;
     moving to Rolle in England, Suso in Germany, Giovanni
     Columbini and Bernard of Siena, and Ludolph of Saxony;
     and continuing to the present age.

124. Constable, Giles. "The Popularity of Twelfth Century
     Spiritual Writers in the Late Middle Ages." *Renais-
     sance Studies in Honor of Hans Baron*. Eds. A. Molho
     and J.A. Tedeschi. DeKalb, Ill.: Northern Illinois
     Univ. Press, 1971, pp. 3-38.

     An exploration of the popularity and influence of
     Anselm, Bernard, Hugh and Richard of St. Victor, and
     William of St. Thierry on 14th- and 15th-century devo-
     tional writing.

125. ———. "Twelfth Century Spirituality and the Late
     Middle Ages." *Medieval and Renaissance Studies*. Ed.
     O.B. Hardison. Chapel Hill: Univ. of North Carolina
     Press, 1971, pp. 27-60.

     In this study Constable illustrates the affinity of
     religious temperaments between the 12th and 15th cen-
     turies, as evinced by the renewed interest by later
     theologians and humanists in such 12th-century spiritual
     writers as Bernard, Anselm, the Victorines, William of
     St. Thierry, and Guigo II of La Chartreuse.

126. Ps.-Dionysius the Areopagite. *On the Divine Names and
     the Mystical Theology*. Trans. C.E. Holt. Translations
     of Christian Literature. Series 1. London: Macmillan
     Co., 1920.

     Translations of two treatises generally attributed to
     Ps.-Dionysius, with two early studies of his thought and
     influence. These treatises are especially important
     because of their relationship to the works of the *Cloud*
     author.

127. Fleming, John V. *An Introduction to the Franciscan
     Literature of the Middle Ages*. Chicago: Franciscan
     Herald Press, 1977.

     Chap. 5, "Bonaventure and the Themes of Franciscan
     Mysticism," fully discusses Bonaventure's centrality to
     later medieval mysticism.

128. Hackett, Peter. "*The Anchoresses' Guide.*" *Month*, N.S.
      23 (1960), 227-40.

      An introduction for the general reader to the *Ancrene
      Riwle*, which Hackett judges to be part of the history
      of English mysticism: "It links traditional and up-to-
      date Continental spirituality with the later English
      mystics; it has its own light hint of mystical possi-
      bility."

129. Hugh of St. Victor. *Selected Spiritual Writings.*
      Trans. A Religious of C.S.M.V., with introduction
      by Aelred Squire. New York and Evanston: Harper and
      Row, 1962.

      Modernized translations from *De Arca Noe Morali*, *De
      Vanitate Mundi*, *The Soul's Three Ways of Seeing* (from
      the *Commentary on Ecclesiastes*), and *De Substantia
      Dilectionis.*

130. ————. *Six Opuscules Spirituels.* With introduction,
      French translation, critical text, and notes by Roger
      Baron. Paris: Les Éditions du Cerf, 1969.

      Includes: *La Méditation*; *La Parole de Dieu*; *La
      Réalité de l'Amour*; *Ce qu'il faut aimer vraiment*; *Les
      Cinq Septenaires*; *Les Sept Dons de l'Esprit-Saint.*

131. Kirchberger, Clare. "Hugh of Saint Victor on the
      Celestial Hierarchy of Denis the Areopagite." *LS*,
      11 (1956), 132-8.

      An extract from Book 6 of Hugh's *Commentary* (Chap. 7
      in Denis), showing Hugh's insistence on love rather than
      knowledge as a means of union and contemplation--a
      departure from Denis which influenced the writers on
      mystical theology in the 12th and succeeding centuries.

132. Knowles, David. "The Influence of Pseudo-Dionysius on
      Western Mysticism." In *Christian Spirituality.* Ed.
      Peter Brooks. London, 1975, pp. 79-94.

      A concise historical analysis of Ps.-Dionysius's place
      in and influence on Western mysticism, with particular
      emphasis on English mysticism.

133. Lawrence, Clifford H., ed. *St. Edmund of Abingdon: A
      Study in Hagiography and History.* Oxford: Clarendon
      Press, 1960.

134.   ————. "Edmund of Abingdon: The *Speculum Ecclesie*."
       Month, 29 (1963), 213-29.

       The life of Edmund as it affected the *Speculum* and an
       analysis of the work as an expression of traditional
       monastic spirituality.

135.   McLoughlin, Justin. "St. Bonaventure and the English
       Mystics." In *S. Bonaventura Grottaferrata, 1274-
       1974*. Vol. II. Rome: Collegio S. Bonaventura, 1974,
       pp. 279-87.

       An exploration of the "kinship of thought" between the
       English mystics and Bonaventure, either directly or
       indirectly, via Augustine and Richard of St. Victor.

136.   A Monk of Parkminster. *Eden's Fourfold River*. London:
       Burns, Oates & Washbourne, Ltd., 1927.

       A modern English translation of this treatise on the
       life of prayer, written for the monks of Witham Charter-
       house c. 1200 and drawn from the *Liber de Quadripertito
       Exercitio Cellae*.

137.   O'Riedl, John. "Bonaventure's Commentary on Dionysius's
       Mystical Theology." *Proceedings of the American
       Catholic Philosophical Association*, 48 (1974), 266-76.

       An examination of the second of Bonaventure's *Colla-
       tions in Hexameron*, with its sustained analysis of Ps.-
       Dionysius's *Mystical Theology*, revealing Bonaventure's
       departures from some of the Ps.-Dionysian teachings,
       such as his different view of the function and efficacy
       of the method of unknowing as an approach to the mystical
       experience.

138.   Richard of St. Victor. *Selected Writings on Contempla-
       tion*. Trans. with introduction and notes by Clare
       Kirchberger. London: Faber and Faber, Ltd., 1957.

       A concise introduction on the place of Richard in the
       development of mystical theology on the Continent and
       in England, with translated portions of *Benjamin Minor,
       Benjamin Major, Of the Four Degrees of Passionate
       Charity*, and shorter extracts. Good basic bibliography
       on Richard.

139.   Ritzke-Rutherford, Jean. *Light and Darkness in Anglo-
       Saxon Thought and Writing*. Frankfurt: Lang Verlag,
       1979.

A study of the influence of Ps.-Dionysius on Anglo-
Saxon spiritual writings, as a part of the English
mystical continuum extending through the 14th and 15th
centuries.

140. Rose, Mary Carmen. "The Maximal Mysticism of Bonaven-
      ture." *Anglican Theological Review*, 59 (1976), 60-75.

      After discussing the element of controversy inherent
      in almost every aspect of mysticism, such as the cogni-
      tive significance of the mystic experience, Rose main-
      tains that "Bonaventure's work provides a perspective
      for the working out of a characterization of mysticism
      in generic terms."

141. Sage, Carleton M. "Miscellany: The Manuscripts of St.
      Aelred." *Catholic Historical Review*, 34 (1948), 437-45.

      A listing of manuscripts of Aelred's ascetic and his-
      torical writings, as a first step towards critical edi-
      tions.

142. Smalley, Beryl. *The Study of the Bible in the Middle
      Ages*. New York: Philosophical Library, 1952.

      An important sub-theme in this scholarly study is the
      relationship of Scripture and biblical exegesis to mys-
      ticism in different historical periods. Excellent in-
      sights into the role of biblical glosses, the use of
      allegory and the spiritual sense of Scripture, through
      the rise of the opinion that reading, even of the Bible,
      was a hindrance to prayer. The end point of the work
      is 1300.

143. Southern, Richard W., ed. *The Life of St. Anselm, Arch-
      bishop of Canterbury, by Eadmer*. London and New York:
      T. Nelson, 1962.

144. Squire, Aelred. "Aelred of Rievaulx and the Monastic
      Tradition Concerning Action and Contemplation." *DR*,
      72 (1954), 289-303.

      An analysis of Aelred's sermons which points to his
      contention that action and contemplation are two ac-
      tivities of a single life and are complementaries in
      the monastic vocation. See also Squire's *Aelred of
      Rievaulx: A Study*. London: SPCK, 1969.

145. Wilmart, André. *Auteurs spirituels et testes dévot du
      moyen âge Latin*. Paris: Bloud et Gay, 1932; 2nd. ed.
      Paris: Études Augustiniennes, 1971.

Studies and critical editions of medieval Latin spiritual writings of Aelred of Rievaulx, Anselm of Canterbury, Bonaventure, Guigo II, Hugh of St. Victor, and William of St. Thierry. The work is concerned more with liturgical and devotional pieces than with mystical works. Provides valuable background on leading predecessors and informing influences on the 14th-century English mystics.

E. GENERAL STUDIES ON THE ENGLISH MYSTICS

146. Ackerman, R.W. "The Liturgical Day in *Ancrene Riwle*." *Speculum*, 53 (1978), 734-44.

    Provides important information for an understanding of the rule and practices of the anchoritic life.

147. Bradley, Ritamary. "Present-Day Themes in the Fourteenth-Century English Mystics." *Spiritual Life*, 20 (1974), 260-7.

    Argues that the medieval mystics may provide an answer to today's revival of interest in mysticism: "From these writers we learn how subjective and collective existence is grounded in immanent and transcendent being--the believer's God, whose power has been brought to the human condition by Jesus."

148. ———. "The English Mystics: A Progress Report on Scholarship and Teaching." *Religious Education*, 73 (1978), 335-45.

    Sets forth the *FCEMN*'s efforts for advancing scholarship in medieval English mysticism, promoting courses in academic curricula, encouraging the editing and publishing of critical and student editions, and concluding with a discussion of new horizons in research in mystical writings.

149. Brégy, Katherine. "The Lady Anchoress." *NCW*, 135 (1932), 9-15.

    Explains the life style of the medieval anchoress, with comments on Rolle and an appreciation of Julian.

150. Bullett, Gerald W. *The English Mystics*. London: Michael Joseph, 1950.

    A series of essays on the English mystics. Chap. 2

concerns Rolle and Julian. Subsequent chapters develop
ideas on later figures, such as George Fox, the Cambridge
Platonists, William Blake, and Wordsworth. According to
Bullett, mysticism is a "sense of apprehension of an im-
mortal reality in and beyond appearance and in oneself."

151. Clay, Rotha M. *The Hermits and Anchorites of England.*
      London: Methuen & Co., Ltd., 1914.

      A history of English recluses through the 16th century,
      with special reference to Rolle and Julian.

152. Coleman, Thomas W. *English Mystics of the Fourteenth
      Century.* Westport, Conn.: Greenwood Press, 1938;
      rpt. 1971.

      A study of the *Ancrene Riwle* and the five leading 14th-
      century mystics. It is written for the general public
      from the standpoint of a Free Churchman. Coleman defines
      the mystic as one who "cultivates communion with God
      with the goal of achieving union." After an excellent
      introduction on the characteristics of Christian mysti-
      cism, Coleman treats of the marks of this distinct
      English group, and then discusses these mystics individual-
      ly and sympathetically.

153. Colledge, E. "The English Mystics and Their Critics."
      LS, 15 (1961), 554-9.

      An objective assessment of David Knowles's findings on
      Augustine Baker, Rolle, the *Cloud*, and the influence of
      the Rhineland mystics on their English contemporaries.
      With Knowles and other critics, Colledge stresses the
      need for critics to have sufficient theological training
      to make correct interpretations of the mystics' writings.

154. ————. "Early English Spirituality." *Month*, 30 (1963),
      108-20.

      A masterful exploration of the origins, derivations,
      and accumulation of English spirituality from early
      Anglo-Saxon times until the Norman invasion, downgrading
      Celtic influence and arguing for a distinctly English
      spiritual ethos.

155. Darwin, Francis D. *The English Mediaeval Recluse.* Lon-
      don: SPCK, 1944.

      After defining the recluse as one who leads the
      anchoritic or enclosed life, as opposed to the hermit,

Darwin presents a concise study of the solitary life, profession, enclosure, and other aspects of anchoritic existence. This work is of special background interest for the lives of Julian and the Continental recluses, supplementing R.M. Clay's *The Hermits and Anchorites of England*.

156. Davis, Charles, ed. *English Spiritual Writers*. New York: Sheed and Ward, 1961.

This book consists of 17 of the 25 articles on the subject of English spirituality published in *Clergy Review* (Nov. 1958-July 1961).

157. Deanesly, Margaret. *The Lollard Bible and Other Medieval Biblical Versions*. Cambridge: Cambridge Univ. Press, 1920.

This study gives substantial notice to such works of medieval mysticism as Rolle's *Psalter*, the *Abbey of the Holy Ghost*, and Hilton's *Epistle on the Mixed Life*. Brief mention is also made of other works of English and Continental mystics. Deanesly supplies some evidence for her statement that the "German mystics of the upper Rhine gave the first important impetus towards the use of vernacular Bibles from the side of orthodoxy."

158. ————. "Vernacular Books in England in the 14th and 15th Centuries." *MLR*, 15 (1920), 349-58.

An assessment of English medieval wills which reveals the booklessness of the population as a whole, the predominance of Latin books over vernacular texts, and the prevalence, in the vernacular corpus, of pious and devotional over secular works.

159. Eaton, M. Eleanor. "The Use of Scripture by the English Mystics." Diss. Stanford Univ. 1954.

Chap. 4 deals directly with the use of Scripture by the English mystics. An appendix lists biblical texts located in Hilton's *Scale*. Other material is useful for an introduction to the English mystics.

160. Gatta, Julie M. "Mind and Mysticism: Uses of the Intellect in the Writings of Three Fourteenth-Century English Mystics." Diss. Cornell Univ. 1978.

An examination of the intellectual dimensions of the *Cloud* author, Hilton, and Julian, as well as the

precedents and backgrounds of the intellectual dimension
within earlier Christian mysticism, and the mystics'
theological congruence with the theology of Thomas
Aquinas.

160a. Glasscoe, Marion, ed. *The Medieval Mystical Tradition
in England*. Exeter: Univ. of Exeter Press, 1980.

This collection of critical essays represents the
proceedings of the Exeter Symposium on the Medieval
Mystical Tradition in England, held in July 1980. The
thirteen studies deal with the five major English
figures and with such related topics as the correspon-
dences between the mystical writings and literary works,
including *Piers Plowman*, the dream visions, and the
drama; the English mystics' participation in the long
continuum of Christian mystical tradition; the religious
milieu and community of belief which the mystics shared
with homiletic and devotional writers; medieval psychology
and the mystics; and new avenues of research on the
mystics.

161. Goyau, Lucie Felix-Faure. "Visions mystique dans
l'Angleterre du moyen âge." *Revue des Deux Mondes*,
16 (1913), 830-56.

A sensitive exploration of Julian's spirituality in
the context of the *Ancrene Riwle* and later Continental
mystics.

162. Hodgson, Geraldine E. *English Mystics*. London: Mowbray
and Co., 1922.

An enlightening study of English mysticism and its
basic characteristics from Anglo-Saxon medieval times,
through the Tractarians and later. Chaps. 2 and 3 con-
cern the great medieval mystics.

163. Hodgson, Phyllis. *Three 14th-Century English Mystics*.
London: Longmans, Green & Co., 1967.

A sound introduction to orthodox Christian mysticism,
with attention given to Rolle, the *Cloud* author, and
Hilton.

164. Inge, William R. *Studies of English Mystics*. London:
John Murray, 1907.

An introduction to the mystics, especially Julian and
Walter Hilton, taken from the St. Margaret's Lectures of
1905.

165. Kendall, Edith L. *A City Not Forsaken: Studies of English Masters of the Spiritual Life*. London: The Faith Press, 1962.

 Includes essays on Rolle (pp. 23-37), Julian (pp. 74-90), and others, and a bibliography.

166. King, Donald P. "The Threefold Way: English Contemplatives in the Fourteenth Century." Diss. Indiana Univ. 1970.

 An analysis of the relationship and reaction of the English mystics--Rolle, the *Cloud* author, Hilton, Julian, Margery Kempe, William Flete, and the Monk of Farne--to the social, religious, and political milieu of the 14th century.

167. Knowles, David. *The Religious Orders in England*. 3 vols. Cambridge: Cambridge Univ. Press, 1948-59.

 These three volumes study the history of religious orders from 1216 until their suppression in England. The material provides an excellent background for the study of the life and times of the medieval mystics. Vol. 2 contains directly pertinent material, such as Chap. 8, "The Spiritual Life of the Fourteenth Century," and Chap. 16, "The Spiritual Life of the Fifteenth Century." All three volumes offer occasional comments on the history of mysticism, such as the notes on the Bridgettine house of Syon.

168. ————. *The English Mystical Tradition*. London: Burns & Oates; and New York: Harper and Brothers, 1961.

 Knowles devotes chapters to the mysticism of Rolle, the *Cloud* author, and Augustine Baker, with critical comments on Baker and his doctrine. He also considers the question of why so many vernacular mystical texts were to be found in 14th-century England.

169. ————. *The Monastic Order in England. A History of its Development from the Times of St. Dunstan to the Fourth Lateran Council, 940-1216*. 2nd ed. Cambridge: Cambridge Univ. Press, 1963.

 Since mystical theology is at times an outcome of monastic experience, this scholarly study of the Benedictines is useful background reading, even though Knowles does not directly treat of mysticism.

170.   ————, and R. Neville Hadcock. *Medieval Religious
        Houses, England and Wales*. London: Longmans, Green
        and Co., 1959.

        A catalogue of religious houses in England and Wales,
        with dates, statistics regarding size, affiliations,
        and other pertinent material.

171.   Leclercq, Jean, François Vandenbroucke, and Louis Bouyer.
        The Spirituality of the Middle Ages. Vol. II of the
        History of Christian Spirituality. London: Burns &
        Oates; and New York: Desclée Co., Inc., 1968.

        Part II, "New Milieux, New Problems, from the Twelfth
        to the Sixteenth Century," concerns Continental and
        English spirituality and mysticism, with English mystics
        discussed on pp. 407-8, 416-28.

172.   MacKinnon, Effie. *Studies in Fourteenth Century English
        Mysticism*. Diss. Univ. of Illinois-Urbana 1934.

        An investigation of the ideas expressed by Rolle,
        Hilton, Julian, and the *Cloud* author to ascertain to
        what degree their mystical theory and practice were
        products of each author's sources and milieu, and to
        what degree they reflected the author's own genius.
        Rolle receives the major emphasis in this study.

173.   Merton, Thomas. *Mystics and Zen Masters*. New York:
        Farrar, Straus and Giroux, 1967.

        The chapter on the English mystics encompasses dis-
        courses on English spirituality, and treats of the major
        14th-century mystics. Merton includes a compendium of
        recent studies and a summary of the main characteristics
        of English mysticism. Recusant mysticism is treated in
        the study on Gertrude More and Augustine Baker.

174.   Owst, Gerald M. *Preaching in Medieval England*. Cam-
        bridge: Cambridge Univ. Press, 1926.

        Although this basic study of sermon literature has
        only passing references to the English mystics, Owst
        evaluates Rolle as "one of the greatest influences in
        our history upon the development of the vernacular
        sermon."

175.   ————. *Literature and Pulpit in Medieval England*.
        Cambridge: Cambridge Univ. Press, 1933.

        This seminal study of the debt of English literature

to the sermons and tractates of the medieval Church
anticipates the present-day resurgence of scholarly
interest in the medieval homiletic tradition and its
relation to devotional, mystical, and literary works.

176. Pantin, William A. *The English Church in the Fourteenth
Century.* Notre Dame, Ind.: Univ. of Notre Dame
Press, 1962.

Concerns selected topics on 14th-century English
Church history, with Part 3 devoted to religious literature, such as instruction manuals for parish priests,
vernacular religious and moral treatises, and English
mystical writings. Pantin emphasizes how the growth of
a literate laity gave rise to this sizeable body of
vernacular writings.

177. Pepler, Conrad. "The Mystical Body in the English
Mystics." *CR*, N.S. 2 (1943), 49-59.

This article assesses the message of the 14th-century
mystics regarding the doctrine of the Mystical Body.
Drawing primarily from Julian's *Revelations*, Pepler
illustrates how Julian and her fellow mystics provide
a synthesis of the two elements of this doctrine: the
external unity of the Church and the internal union of
all faithful with Christ. Thus Pepler feels the mystics
speak not only to their age, but also to ours.

178. —————. "The Way of Perfection in the English Mystics."
LS, 1 (1946), 1-9, 43-7, 78-83, 136-41.

This substantial series takes as its premise that the
English mystics provide "the best material for Ascetico-
Mystical study in the English tongue." In his consideration of *Piers Plowman*, Pepler shows how faith is used
to imply purification, and therefore is the first step
towards the sphere in which lies the Beatific Vision.

179. —————. "The English Spirit." *LS*, 11 (1956), 52-65.

A distillation of the English spirit and spirituality
from its Celtic, Roman, Anglo-Saxon, and Anglo-Norman
origins, with exemplars from monastic figures and
mystical writers.

180. —————. *The Three Degrees: A Study of Christian Mysticism.* St. Louis: Herder, 1957.

An investigation designed to recall the modern

enthusiasts for mystics to the foundation of true
Christian mysticism. Of special interest is Chap. 15,
"English Mysticism."

181.   ————. *The English Religious Heritage*. St. Louis:
        Herder, 1958.

        An introduction to the growth of the spiritual life
        in England during the later Middle Ages up to the 15th
        century. Includes the English mystics, and stresses
        ascetic and mystical theology. These essays were
        originally published in *Life of the Spirit*.

182.   Petry, Ray C. "Social Responsibility and the Late
        Medieval Mystics." *Church History*, 21 (1952), 3-19.

        Argues that the great mystics participated in the
        affairs of the world and cared for the needs of others,
        as proven by Meister Eckhart, Tauler, Rolle, Ruysbroeck,
        the *Cloud* author, and others. Also see Richard Kieck-
        hefer, "Mysticism and Social Consciousness in the Four-
        teenth Century," *University of Ottawa Quarterly*, 48
        (1978), which amplifies Petry's findings.

183.   Renaudin, Paul. *Quatre Mystiques Anglais*. Paris:
        Éditions du Cerf, 1945.

        An insightful study of Rolle, Julian, Gertrude More,
        and Augustine Baker, with a rather sharp criticism of
        Baker.

184.   Riehle, Wolfgang. "Der Seelengründ in der englischen
        Mystik des Mittelalters im Vergleich zur deutschen."
        Grossbritannien und Deutschland. Ed. O. Kuhn.
        Munich: Goldmann, 1975, pp. 461-76.

        The intention of this study is to disprove the position,
        long held by German scholars, that English mystical
        writings derived basically from the German mystical
        texts. Riehle concludes that both German and English
        vernacular mysticism are marked by a return to Latin
        mysticism and to scholasticism, which produces misleading
        similarities. Riehle also deals fully with the metaphor
        of the ground of the soul.

185.   Ryder, Andrew. "The English Spiritual Writers of the
        Fourteenth Century. I. The Writers and Their Back-
        ground." *Mount Carmel*, 26 (1979), 199-209.

        The first part of a continuing study, presenting an

overview of the historical events and the status of the
Church and State in 14th-century England. Also included
is basic information on the lives and writings of Rolle,
the *Cloud* author, Hilton, and Julian.

186. ————. "The English Spiritual Writers of the Fourteenth
Century. II. The Sources of Their Teaching." *Mount
Carmel*, 27 (1979), 25-34.

Shows ways in which the same four authors reflect the
influences of the Scriptures, the Fathers of the Church,
Ps.-Dionysius, and Franciscan and Dominican spirituality.
Julian is cited for her striking originality, and is
contrasted with the great Continental women mystics of
the same century.

187. ————. "The English Spiritual Writers of the Fourteenth
Century. III. Our Knowledge of God." *Mount Carmel*,
27 (1979), 72-82.

A consideration of the degree to which the medieval
English mystics thought it possible to know the divine
essence in this life. Ryder also compares their writings
with Ps.-Dionysius's *Mystical Theology* to see whether
they prescribed the cataphatic or apophatic approach to
the *via mystica*, and concludes that only the *Cloud*
author followed the negative way.

188. ————. "The English Spiritual Writers of the Fourteenth
Century. IV." *Mount Carmel*, 27 (1979), 138-48.

This article examines the relationship between nature
and grace in mystical theology. Ryder argues that,
while only Julian is concerned in any way with meta-
physical theology, all of the mystics give practical
advice concerning the natures of sin and man. This
advice springs from an optimistic view of the significance
of the Fall, and of man's nature.

189. ————. "The English Spiritual Writers of the Fourteenth
Century. V." *Mount Carmel*, 27 (1979), 192-203.

This essay considers the theme of the stages of mystical experience. Ryder finds Hilton to have the most
completely developed system, while Rolle, the *Cloud*
author, and Julian are more concerned with the ultimate
experience than with the preparatory stages. The study
concludes with a brief comparison of the English and
Carmelite mystics.

190.   ————. *Love Is His Way. Reflections on the Theme of*
        Love in Christian Literature. Belfast: Christian
        Journals Limited, 1979.

        An examination of the mystical life of love followed
        by six mystics from three different cultural backgrounds:
        medieval England (Richard Rolle and Julian of Norwich);
        the Spanish Golden Age (Teresa of Avila and John of the
        Cross); and late 19th-century France (Thérèse of Lisieux
        and Leo Dehon).

191.   Spurgeon, Caroline F. *Mysticism in English Literature.*
        Cambridge: Cambridge Univ. Press; and New York: G.P.
        Putnam's Sons, 1913; rpt. 1922.

        Spurgeon writes with warmth and appreciation of Rolle,
        Julian, and Hilton, stressing the centrality of love in
        their writings. Her objective is to characterize the
        many English writers whose "inmost principle is rooted
        in mysticism, or whose work is on the whole so permeated
        by mystical thought that their attitude of mind is not
        fully understood apart from it." Accordingly, she in-
        cludes Love and Beauty Mystics, Nature Mystics,
        Philosophical Mystics, as well as the Devotional and
        Religious Mystics.

192.   Thompson, E. Margaret. *The Carthusian Order in England.*
        London: SPCK; New York and Toronto: Macmillan Co.,
        1930.

        A history of the Carthusian order, its monasteries,
        and its importance to English history, culture, and
        mystical tradition in the early and late Middle Ages.

193.   Thornton, Martin. *English Spirituality.* London: SPCK,
        1963.

        A comprehensive assessment of the origins, backgrounds,
        and characteristics of English ascetical theology, "ac-
        cording to the English pastoral tradition," with an en-
        lightening and, at times, provocative discussion of the
        English mystics (Chaps. 13-18).

194.   Tuma, George W. *The Fourteenth-Century English Mystics:*
        A Comparative Analysis. 2 vols. Elizabethan and
        Renaissance Studies 61 and 62. Salzburg, 1977.

        Using a literary approach, Tuma considers the concepts
        of purgation, illumination, and mystic union as they occur
        in the writings of the medieval mystics. Excellent
        bibliography.

195. Walsh, James, ed. *Pre-Reformation English Spirituality.*
      New York: Fordham Univ. Press, 1965.

      An assessment of English spirituality with its stress
      on eremetical life, spiritual orthodoxy, and its synthesis
      of the active and contemplative life, with the latter
      predominating. Presented as a series of essays, moving
      from Bede to early and late medieval spiritual writers,
      and ending with Benet of Canfield and Augustine Baker.

196. Watkin, E.I. *Poets and Mystics.* London and New York:
      Sheed and Ward, 1953.

      Contains excellent re-workings of earlier essays on
      Julian of Norwich (published in *The English Way*); Margery
      Kempe (published in *DR*); and Dom Augustine Baker (pub-
      lished in *Great Catholics* and *DR*). The Julian and Kempe
      essays also appear in *On Julian of Norwich and In Defence
      of Margery Kempe.* Exeter: Univ. of Exeter Press, 1979.

197. Wilson, R.M. *The Lost Literature of Medieval England.*
      2nd ed. London, 1952; rev. London: Methuen & Co., 1970.

      Chap. 8, "Religious and Didactic Literature," shows
      evidence of manuscripts of this category in wills and
      monastic library catalogues.

                  F. LITERARY CRITICISM AND THE MYSTICS

           Middle English prose texts, and especially
           religious works, have long been treated as pre-
           dominantly informative, didactic, and unliter-
           ary, thereby not receiving critical scrutiny,
           except perhaps by dialectologists or an oc-
           casional rhetorician. They remain, for the
           most part, an amorphous link between Old and
           Modern English language and literature.
           Furthermore, little attention has been paid
           to the impact of this religious corpus on the
           secular literature and drama of the period,
           to the translation process which produced a
           large part of it, and even less to a clarifying
           organizational schema. The works of the mys-
           tics have fared somewhat better and in fact as
           evinced by the following studies, are helping
           to solve some of the above problems and to
           point the way for further fruitful research in

such areas as stylistic analysis, metaphorical
language, intended audience, and informing
influence of the visual arts and literature.

198. Alford, John A. "Hawkyn's Coat: Some Observations om
      Piers Plowman B. XIV. 22-7." *MA*, 43 (1974), 133-7.

Relates Julian's parable of the Lord and servant to a
passage in *Piers Plowman*, which seems to be an allusion
to Matt. 6: 19-20, concerning the metaphor of garments,
first stained and then transformed, for the soul.

199. Ashley, Kathleen M. "The Specter of Bernard's Noonday
      Demon in Medieval Drama." *ABR*, 30 (1979), 205-21.

This article examines the Bernardian concept of the
"noonday demon" as it appears in the writings of such
14th and 15th century mystics as Birgitta of Sweden,
Margery Kempe, the *Cloud* author's translation of
Richard of St. Victor's *Benjamin Minor*, and Jean Gerson,
and argues that the concept's popularization by the
mystics resulted in its incorporation in the York and
Towneley mystery cycles.

200. Blake, Norman F. *Middle English Religious Prose.* York
      Medieval Texts. London: Edward Arnold; and Evanston,
      Ill.: Northwestern Univ. Press, 1972.

Blake surveys style in Middle English religious prose,
and studies the distinction between prose and verse in
that body of literature. He also provides an analysis
of the religious and literary aspects of such works as
Hali Meiðhad, *The Wooing of Our Lord*, *The Abbey of the
Holy Ghost*, and *Epistle of Discretion of Stirrings*.
The great works of the 14th-century mystics are not
included.

201. ————. "Middle English Prose and its Audience."
      Anglia, 90 (1972), 437-55.

Projects a categorization of Middle English prose
writings on the basis of the intended audience for those
works.

202. ————. "*The Form of Living* in Prose and Poetry."
      Archiv, 211 (1974), 300-8.

A study of poetic versions of mystical prose works,
from which the mystical elements have been excised for
a more general audience. Cites Rolle's *Form of Living*

and the *Mirror of St. Edmund* as examples, and encourages
further investigation of other poetic adaptations of
prose texts.

203.   ――――. "Varieties of Middle English Religious Prose."
        In *Chaucer and Middle English Studies in Honour of
        Rossell Hope Robbins.* Ed. Beryl Rowland. London:
        George Allen and Unwin, 1974, pp. 348-56.

        Blake differentiates Middle English religious prose
        on the basis of the purpose for which a particular text
        was written, since that purpose will often determine
        the form and approach of the prose, as its most important
        feature.

204.   ――――. "The English Language in Medieval Literature."
        Studia Neophilologica, 48 (1976), 59-75.

        Posits that, owing to the close relationship between
        literature and language in the medieval period, the
        teaching of medieval literature cannot be divorced from
        the linguistic conditions which produced it. Some
        examples are chosen from devotional literature.

205.   Chambers, R.W. *On the Continuity of English Prose from
        Alfred to More and His School.* London, 1932. First
        printed as an introduction to *Harpsfield's Life of
        More.* Ed. E.V. Hitchcock and R.W. Chambers. EETS
        O.S. 186. London, 1931. Also printed in EETS O.S.
        191A, 1932, 1966.

        Discusses in part the contributions of the 14th-century
        mystics to the English prose tradition, citing the
        Ancrene Riwle, Hilton's and Rolle's works, and *The Cloud
        of Unknowing.*

206.   Clark, Cecily. "Early Middle English Prose: Three
        Essays in Stylistics." *EIC,* 18 (1968), 361-82.

        Proposes careful syntactic, stylistic, and lexical
        approaches to Middle English prose to recreate, if pos-
        sible, the author's intention and audience response.
        Clark's analyses of the *Katherine Group, Ancrene Wisse,*
        and *The Peterborough Chronicle* are pertinent and in-
        structive for similar critical investigations of Middle
        English devotional and mystical texts.

207.   Crean, John E. "Studies in Fourteenth Century Mystical
        Terminology: The Middle High German of Meister Eckhart

and the Middle Netherlandic of Jan van Ruusbroec."
Diss. Yale Univ. 1966.

Isolates and compares six significant mystical stem
words common to a major High and Low German mystic of
the 14th century, and concludes that Ruysbroeck's
writings prove to be superior to Eckhart's in quantity
of diverse forms, depth of semantic field, and clarity
of expression.

207a. Davis, Walter R. "Homily and Poem: Doctrine and Form."
      Notre Dame English Journal, 12 (1980), 101-11.

      Davis explores the interaction of religion and litera-
      ture, as shown by two approaches: homiletic/historical,
      dealing with the author's situation, audience, aims, and
      method; and literary/ahistorical, which stresses the
      work's formal qualities. He concludes: "to perceive the
      form or structure in an authentic religious work is to
      experience a central fact about spiritual reality."

208. Diemer, P. "Langland and Spiritual Renewal." *Cistercian*
      Studies, 13 (1978), 167-76.

      An assessment of *Piers Plowman* in its 14th-century
      context, which concludes that "the whole character of
      the man [Langland], together with his 'down to earth'
      style, link him closely in one's mind to the group we
      call the English mystics."

209. Doyle, Teresa A. "Classical and Baroque Elements of
      Spirituality in Medieval Didactic Works for Women."
      Diss. Fordham Univ. 1948.

210. Dunn, Catherine. "Popular Devotion in the Vernacular
      Drama of Medieval England." *Medievalia et Humanistica*,
      4 (1973), 55-68.

      Dunn sees the vernacular drama as another step in the
      process of translation into the national linguistic
      idiom, and finds that many of the expansions of the
      liturgical dramatic core reveal a strong measure of
      affective spirituality akin to that of Rolle.

211. Ewer, Mary A. *A Survey of Mystical Symbolism*. London:
      SPCK; and New York: Macmillan Co., 1933.

      An exploration of the mystics' characteristic sym-
      bolic language, defined as an expression, by means of
      analogy, of experiences and ideas not directly and

literally expressible in words. Ewer's survey attempts
"to show the relationships of different types of
symbolism to each other and to the subject of mysticism
as a whole." Ewer finds that all types of mysticism
are united by the fact of a conscious relationship between the soul and some overwhelmingly greater Unity.
Significant points of her discussion cover the language
of the spiritual senses, spiritual progress, mystical
evaluation, mysteries, and mystical union.

212. Finnegan, Jeremy. "'Similitudes' in the Writing of
      Saint Gertrude of Helfta." *MS*, 19 (1957), 48-54.

      An examination of how the rhetorical figure of the
      "similitude" in Gertrude's writings, particularly the
      Legatus Divinae Pietatis, or *Revelations*, records the
      customs, occupations, and human ideals of her day, both
      within the cloister and without. Of interest to students
      of the language of the mystics.

213. Gauvin, C. "The Mystics and the Religious Theater in
      England at the End of the Middle Ages." *VS*, 131
      (1977), 716-29.

      Contends that the English medieval religious theater
      bears the marks of a sensitivity to the writings on the
      Passion also found in Rolle, Julian, and Margery Kempe.

214. Gehring, Hester McNeal Reed. "The Language of Mysticism
      in South German Dominican Convent Chronicles of the
      Fourteenth Century." Diss. Univ. of Michigan 1957.

      This study attempts to determine what contributions
      were made by the chronicles to the language of medieval
      German mysticism. It also considers the background of
      the chronicles--literary, social, and religious--and
      interprets the mystic concepts which the terminology is
      used to depict.

215. Gish, Nancy K. "The Significance of the Mystic in T.S.
      Eliot's Theme of Time." In *Studies in Medieval
      Culture*, VI and VII. Eds. John R. Sommerfeldt and
      E. Roxanne Elder. The Medieval Institute. Kalamazoo,
      Mich.: Western Michigan Univ., 1976, pp. 169-76.

      Examines the use of the mystical writings of Julian
      of Norwich and John of the Cross in *Four Quartets*.

216. Harris, Mary E. "The Word in the Wilderness: Style in
      English Anchoritic Prose." Diss. Univ. of California,

Berkeley 1970.

Discusses the development of eremetic life from 3rd-
century Egypt to 15th-century England, and analyzes
stylistically Aelred of Rievaulx's *De Institutione
Inclusarum*, *Ancrene Riwle*, and Rolle's *Form of Living*.
Harris feels that these three works, all addressed to
female recluses, constitute the core of medieval anchoritic
prose, and influenced the course of English prose because
of their personal tone and flexible style.

217. Hirsh, John C. "The Experience of God: A New Classifi-
      cation of Certain Late Medieval Affective Texts."
      Chaucer Review, 11 (1976), 11-21.

      Adopting Joachim Wach's criteria of religious ex-
      perience, Hirsh delineates three categories of affective
      writings: texts of encounter, evincing direct religious
      experience; texts of adoration, emphasizing the ex-
      perience of apprehending Christ rather than the fact of
      the apprehension; and texts of devotion. These categories
      are offered to promote the examination of affective
      devotional texts.

218. Homier, Donald F. "The Function of Rhetoric in Sug-
      gesting Stages of Contemplation in the Vernacular
      Writings of the Fourteenth-Century English Mystics."
      Diss. Northern Illinois Univ. 1975.

      An examination of the relationship between rhetoric
      and subject matter in vernacular mystical writings on
      contemplation by the major 14th-century English mystics.

219. Hussey, S.S. "Langland, Hilton, and the Three Lives."
      RES, N.S. 7 (1956), 132-50.

      A thoughtful consideration of Langland's terms of
      Dowell, Dobet, and Dobest in *Piers Plowman* in the light
      of Hilton's active, contemplative, and mixed lives, as
      well as the contemplative triad of Purgation, Illumina-
      tion, and Unity.

220. Kinney, Thomas L. "English Verse of Complaint, 1250-
      1400." Diss. Univ. of Michigan 1959.

      Identifies the complaint as a type of verse which
      differs from didacticism and satire, which is marked by
      skill and imagination, and which furnishes insight into
      other literature of the period--Rolle, Wyclif, Langland,
      and Gower.

221. Knight, John Howard. "Mysticism in Sir Thomas Malory's Grail." Diss. Univ. of Notre Dame 1979.

  The author contends that critical scholarship has overlooked Malory's Grail story as a storehouse of mystical doctrines, despite its reliance on the French mystical allegory *Queste del Saint Graal*. Knight says that Malory was aware of these French mystical doctrines and incorporated them into his story in order to establish its ethical perspective.

222. Lüers, Grete. *Die Sprache der deutschen Mystik des Mittelalters im Werke der Mechthild von Magdeburg*. München: Unveränderter reprografischer Nachdruck der Ausg., 1926; rpt. Darmstadt: Wissenschaftliche Buchgesellschaft, 1966.

  An analysis of Mechthild's metaphoric language, with an alphabetical register of terms and motifs used by Mechthild and other Continental mystics.

223. Maryanna, Sr. "Charged with a Strong Flame: The Prose of Julian of Norwich." *The Magnificat*, 77 (1945-6), 6-11.

  A discussion of the importance of the English mystics, and especially Julian, to the development of English prose.

224. Morgan, Margery. "A Treatise in Cadence." *MLR*, 47 (1952), 156-84.

  A stylistic discussion of the precise meaning of "cadence," as it occurs in the preface to *A Talking of the Love of God*, as well as in the work itself and other 14th-century Middle English prose writings. Drawing on Latin rhetorical *dictamen*, Morgan identifies cadence as rhetorical punctuation, i.e., a guide to intonation, which, with writers such as Rolle, produces what appears to be snatches of verse. Morgan shows the importance of manuscript punctuation, and posits that cadence, along with other stylistic features, indicates a distinct school of 14th-century writers of devotional prose.

225. ———. "*A Talking of the Love of God* and the Continuity of Stylistic Tradition in Middle English Prose Meditations." *RES*, N.S. 3 (1952), 97-116.

  Morgan develops connections between *A Talking of the Love of God* and other works, including the *Ancrene Riwle*,

on grounds of date, dialect, and general spirit, and
also notes stylistic similarities with the prose of
Richard Rolle.

226. Munson, Miriam. "Humility, Charity, and the Beatitudes
      in *Patience* and *The Scale of Perfection*." *FCEMN*, 4/3
      (1978), 17-22.

      A thoughtful comparison of the use of the Beatitudes
      in *Patience* and the *Scale*, which points to both authors'
      basic concern with the pursuit of virtue, but stipulates
      that only Hilton is concerned with the contemplative
      life. Thus she argues against the interpretation of
      Patience as a parable of the contemplative life, proposed
      by John T. Irwin and T.D. Kelly, "The Way and the End Are
      One: *Patience* as a Parable of the Contemplative Life."
      ABR, 25 (1974), 33-55.

227. Nolan, Barbara. *The Gothic Visionary Perspective*.
      Princeton: Princeton Univ. Press, 1977.

      Nolan contends that "Gothic visionary art was essen-
      tially an art of edification in the root sense of that
      word: the formal construction was to effect spiritual
      reconstruction, reshaping the souls of observers within
      the patterns of sacred history in order to transport
      them even before death into the company of the saved."
      She traces this Gothic visionary perspective from
      religious writers and artists of the 12th and early 13th
      centuries, such as Richard of St. Victor, and shows how
      they affected the shape of literary narrative and
      religious art for two centuries, with the major portion
      of her literary discussion centered on Dante, the *Pearl*,
      and Langland.

228. Osberg, Richard H. "The Alliterative Theory and
      Thirteenth-Century Devotional Prose." *JEGP*, 76 (1977),
      40-54.

      Osberg argues that the alliterative lyrics were not
      influenced particularly by the romances of the allitera-
      tive revival, but that Old English alliteration was
      channeled into the lyric through Middle English devo-
      tional prose.

229. Patterson, Lee W. "Ambiguity and Interpretation: A
      Fifteenth Century Reading of *Troilus and Criseyde*."
      Speculum, 54 (1979), 297-330.

      A hypothesis on the medieval experience of reading

Troilus and Criseyde, based on the incorporation of a
passage from the *Troilus* (lines 400-6) into the *Disce
Mori*, and resting on the *amor/amicitia* topos as delinea-
ted in David of Augsburg's *Formula Novitiorum*, Gerard of
Liège's *De Doctrine Cordis*, and Aelred of Rievaulx's
De Spirituali Amicitia and *Speculum Caritatis*.

230. Riehle, Wolfgang. *Studien zur englischen Mystik des
      Mittelalters unter besonderer Berücksichtigung ihrer
      Metaphorik*. Heidelberg: Carl Winter Universitäts-
      verlag, 1977.

      A seminal comparative and stylistic assessment of 14th-
      century English mystical writings, supplemented by such
      precedent works as the *Ancrene Riwle* and the Wooing
      Group, and by Middle English translations of Continental
      works. In addition to a systematic exploration of both
      predominant metaphors and mystical terminology, Riehle
      assesses the homogeneity of the English mystical works,
      stylistic interrelations within this group, and the
      question of Continental influence.

231. Salter, Elizabeth. "Ludolphus of Saxony and His English
      Translators." *MA*, 33 (1964), 26-35.

      A discussion of two Middle English translations of
      Ludolph of Saxony's *Vita Christi*, one by John Fewterer
      of Syon Abbey, and a second anonymous rendering from a
      15th-century French version by Guillaume le Menand.

232. ————. *Nicholas Love's Myrrour of the Blessed Lyf of
      Jesu Christ*. Analecta Cartusiana No. 10. Salzburg,
      1974.

      A comprehensive analysis of Love's work, including a
      long chapter on "The English Tradition of Prose Transla-
      tion," and considerable commentary on the entire canon
      of English spiritual writings.

233. Smedick, Louis. "*A Talkyng of þe Loue of God* and the
      Rhythm of Meditation." Diss. Bryn Mawr College 1967.

      Discusses the elements responsible for the development
      of the vernacular prose lyric, and concludes that the
      rhythm of *A Talking* springs from the meditational pur-
      pose of the work, rather than from stylistic influence
      upon the author, with the stanzaic structure reflecting
      the pattern of the meditating mind.

234. ————. "Cursus in Middle English: *A Talkyng of þe
      Loue of God* Reconsidered." *MS*, 37 (1975), 387-405.

Smedick joins those critics who hold that the so-
called cursus in Old English is nothing more than a
part of the natural rhythm of the language, and thus
opposes Margery Morgan's assertion that the rhythm of
A Talking may be partly in imitation of the Latin
cursus.

235.   ————. "Parallelism and Pointing in Rolle's Rhythmical
       Style." *MS*, 41 (1979), 404-67.

Through a study of medieval punctuation, Smedick
arrives at a description of the aural character and
meditational tone of Rolle's English prose style,
especially as revealed through parallelism. She finds
the practice of eight representative scribes to be
remarkably consistent. The passages analyzed are from
the "Amore langueo" section of the *Form of Living*. A
Catalogue of Signs is appended, containing definitions
and variants for the principal forms of medieval punctuation.

236.   Sticca, Sandro. "Drama and Spirituality in the Middle
       Ages." *Medievalia et Humanistica*, 4 (1973), 68-87.

The author believes that literary historians have
been reticent in ascertaining the importance of medieval
spirituality in the inception and development of medieval
drama. He points not only to Hrotswitha, but also to
the influence of the Christocentric mysticism of Bonaventure, Anselm, and Bernard on the dramatization of
Christ's Passion. A companion study is *"Officium
Passionis Domini*: An Unpublished Manuscript of the
14th Century." *Franciscan Studies*, 34 (1974), 144-99,
stressing the literary, dramatic, liturgical, and
iconographical consequences of Franciscan mystical and
devotional writings dealing with the suffering Redeemer.

237.   Stone, Robert K. *Middle English Prose Style: Margery
       Kempe and Julian of Norwich*. The Hague and Paris:
       Mouton, 1970.

A pioneer assessment of the prose style of these two
English mystics, with introduction, critical notes, and
bibliography. Of special worth are the sections dealing
with classified lists of imagery, rhythm, and rhyme.

238.   Wakelin, M.F. "Richard Rolle and the Language of
       Mystical Experience in the Fourteenth Century." *DR*,
       97 (1979), 192-203.

While primarily concerned with Rolle, Wakelin also
uses the writings of Hilton, Julian, and the *Cloud*
author to describe how the mystics broke through the
"linguistic impasse" of communicating what is essentially incommunicable, relying heavily on love imagery.

239. Whitman, J.H.M. "Thoughts on the Art of Mystical
      Description." *Studia Mystica*, 1 (1978), 59-73.

      A cogent examination of the difficulties in coping
      linguistically with the mystical experience.

240. Wilson, Richard M. "Three Middle English Mystics."
      In *Essays and Studies for Members of the English
      Association*, N.S. 9 (1956), 87-112.

      Deals with Rolle, Julian, and Margery Kempe, not
      primarily from a religious point of view, but from
      their position as writers of English prose. Wilson
      also traces the tradition, sources, and milieu which
      produced this flowering of English mysticism. He con-
      cludes that Julian was the greatest of the Middle
      English mystics, "unique in that she combines the fervor
      of the Continental women mystics with the sanity and
      balance characteristic of English mysticism, and this
      again with the speculativeness of the Continental men
      writers of her day."

241. ————. "On the Continuity of English Prose." In
      *Mélanges de linguistique et de philologie. Fernand
      Mossé in Memoriam*. Paris: Didier, 1959.

      Wilson criticizes R.W. Chambers's thesis on the role
      of devotional literature in the history of English
      prose, but argues for the importance of the *Ancrene
      Riwle* in the continuity between Old and Middle English
      prose.

242. Workman, Samuel K. *Fifteenth Century Translation as
      an Influence on English Prose*. Princeton: Princeton
      Univ. Press, 1940; rpt. New York: Octagon Books, 1972.

      An insightful study which deals with the translations
      of several of the mystics--including Rolle, Suso,
      Birgitta of Sweden, and which points the way for
      further study in this area.

243. Zeeman, Elizabeth. "Nicholas Love--A Fifteenth Century
      Translator." *RES*, N.S. 6,. No. 22 (1955), 113-27.

      A study of Love's *Mirror of the Blessed Life of*

Jesus Christ in terms of its author, sources, audience, and the contribution made by Love and other medieval translators to the general development of English prose.

244.   ————. "Continuity in Middle English Devotional
        Prose." *JEGP*, 55 (1956), 417-22.

A study of Middle English devotional prose, enlarging on R.W. Chambers's "continuity" thesis to include the important shift of emphasis in writings from West to East in England.

245.   ————. "Continuity and Change in Middle English Ver-
        sions of the *Meditationes Vitae Christi*." *MA*, 26
        (1957), 25-31.

This report represents the first step in a study of the relationship of Nicholas Love's *Mirror* to several Middle English translations of the *Meditationes*, with the comparison revealing Love's great skill and stylistic excellence as a translator.

246.   ————. "*Piers Plowman* and the Pilgrimage to Truth."
        In *Middle English Survey*. Ed. Edward Vasta. Notre
        Dame, Ind.: Univ. of Notre Dame Press, 1965, pp. 195-
        215.

Pointing to the links between the development of the allegory in *Piers* and mystical processes, Zeeman shows how the writings of the 14th-century English mystics clarify some of Langland's leading concepts and aims.

II. RICHARD ROLLE OF HAMPOLE
1300?-1349

Richard Rolle was one of the best-known and
most prolific writers among the English
mystics. This section of the bibliography
considers:
A. Rolle's genuine canon, which is divided
   into his Latin and English works, as well
   as his English lyrics.
B. Anthologies of Rolle's Latin and English
   works.
C. Spurious or Doubtful Works.
D. Biographical Studies.
E. General Critical Studies.

A. ROLLE'S GENUINE CANON

A1. LATIN WORKS: *Canticum Amoris, Judica Me Deus, Melos
   Amoris (Melum Contemplativorum), Job, Canticles, Super
   Threnos, Super Apocalypsim, Super Orationem Dominicam,
   Super Symbolum Apostolorum, Super Mulierem Fortem, De Dei
   Misericordia, Latin Psalter, Super Psalmum, Contra Amatores
   Mundi (Liber de Amore Dei Contra Amatores Mundi), Super
   Magnificat* (in Latin and English), *Incendium Amoris, De
   Emendatione Vitae.*

Canticum Amoris

247. Liegey, Gabriel M. "The *Canticum Amoris* of Richard
     Rolle." *Traditio,* 12 (1956), 369-91.

     A thorough discussion of the *Canticum Amoris*, with its
     Marian exmphasis, including an examination of diction,
     versification, and other stylistic considerations.
     Liegey disagrees with Hope Emily Allen's statement that
     after the *Canticum*, Rolle's devotion to the Blessed
     Virgin Mary languished. Also included is a critical
     edition of the poem, based on MS. Trinity College,
     Dublin, 153.

248. Wilmart, André. "Le *Cantique d'amour* de Richard Rolle."
      Revue d'Ascetique et de Mystique, 21 (1940), 131-48.

      An introduction to the poem, noting the verse form,
      pattern of images, use of alliteration, all of which are
      subordinated to the primary matter of the poem--a genuine
      mystical witness to Rolle's ecstasy. Includes an edition
      of the *Canticum*, based on MSS. Oxford, Bodleian Library,
      Rawlinson C. 397 and Trinity College, Dublin, 153.

Judica Me Deus

249. Daly, John Philip. "An Edition of the *Judica Me Deus*
         of Richard Rolle." Diss. Univ. of North Carolina
         1961.

      A critical text of this work, based on the 17 extant
      manuscripts. The introduction deals with the manu-
      scripts and their relationships, the indebtedness of the
      work to the *Oculi Sacerdotis* (*Pars Oculi*) of William of
      Pagula, and dating factors.

Melos Amoris (*Melum Contemplativorum*)

250. Arnould, Emile F.J., ed. *The Melos Amoris of Richard
         Rolle of Hampole.* Oxford: Basil Blackwell, 1957.

      An excellent assessment of prior scholarship on Rolle,
      plus a synopsis of the *Melos*'s main topics, illustrative
      quotations from other works of Rolle, and an exemplar
      critical edition of the *Melos*. See John H. Fisher's
      review in *Speculum*, 33 (1958), 373-5, criticizing the
      lack of an English translation, as well as Arnould's
      stand on such scholarly issues as Rolle's inimical
      attitude toward ecclesiastical authorities and his
      priesthood.

251. Liegey, Gabriel. "The Rhetorical Aspects of Richard
         Rolle's *Melos Contemplativorum*." Diss. Columbia Univ.
         1954.

      According to Liegey, the *Melos* is a work of mystical
      literature, which reflects Rolle's wide knowledge of
      Scripture, ascetical and mystical writings, and contem-
      porary life. Liegey cites repetition as the work's
      main fault, and examines the alliteration, figurative
      language, paradox, and other stylistic features which
      influenced devotional literature down to Herbert, Donne,
      and Crashaw.

252. ————. "Richard Rolle's 'Carmen Prosaicum,' an Edition
     and Commentary." *MS*, 19 (1957), 15-36.

     A discussion of the extraction of the "Carmen" from
     the *Melos Amoris*, and of Rolle's fusion of native
     English alliterative and Latin poetics, plus a critical
     edition of the work.

253. Vandenbroucke, François, ed. *Le chant d'amour (Melos
     Amoris)*. Trans. Les Moniales de Wisques from the Latin
     text of E.J.F. Arnould's edition. 2 vols. in 1.
     Paris: Les Editions du Cerf, 1971.

     Vandenbroucke provides a thorough introduction to
     Rolle and his works, the critical problems of the *Melos*,
     stylistic considerations, psychological insights into
     Rolle's character afforded by the *Melos*, and the contem-
     plative experience represented in the work. There is a
     facing Latin version and French translation. See Francis
     Rapp's review in *Rev. Hist. Spir.*, 53 (1977), 343-5,
     pointing to the significance of the *Melos* as a witness
     to 14th-century spirituality, and commending Vanden-
     broucke's astute analysis of the author and his work.

Job

254. *Explanationes in Job*. Oxford: Theodoric Rood, 1483?
     (Note: A rhymed Middle English version, "Pety Iob,"
     drawn from Rolle's treatise and ascribed possibly to
     Richard Maidestone, is in H 2, pp. 380-9.)

Commentary on the Canticles

255. Madon, Y. "Le *Commentaire* de Richard Rolle sur les
     premiers versets du *Cantique des Cantiques*." *Mélanges
     de Sciences Religieuses*, 7 (1950), 311-25.

     An edition of Rolle's Latin *Commentary on the Canticle
     of Canticles*, drawn from MS. Bodl. 861 and collated
     with MSS. Corpus Christi College 193, Bodl. Laud 528,
     B·.L. Harl. 5235 and Vesp. E. I, with facing French
     translation.

256. Murray, Elizabeth M. "Richard Rolle's *Commentary on the
     Canticles* Edited from MS. Trinity College, Dublin,
     153." Diss. Fordham Univ. 1958.

257. Wilmart, André. "Richard Rolle sur le Nom de Jesus."
     In *Le "Jubilus" dit de Saint Bernard*. Rome: Edizioni

di Storia e Letteratura, 1944, 272-80.

Wilmart believes that Rolle's *Oleum Effusum* (*Encomium Nominis Jesu*) shows the influence of the *Jubilus*. (Note: A Middle English translation of the *Encomium* is in H 1, pp. 186-92.)

Super Apocalypsim

258. Marzac, Nicole, ed. *Richard Rolle de Hampole (1300-1349): Vie et oeuvres suivies du tractatus Super Apocalypsim*. Paris: Librairie Philosophique J. Vrin, 1968.

An exhaustive study of Rolle's life, based on available documents, his influence on Julian of Norwich and Hilton, a survey of his works, including manuscripts and critical editions, a study of Rolle's sources and doctrines, and a critical edition of the text with facing French translation.

Latin Psalter

259. Porter, Mary Louise. "*Latin Commentary on the Psalms*." Diss. Cornell Univ. 1929.

A study of Rolle's life and works, together with a critical edition of the *Commentary*.

Super Psalmum

260. Dolan, James C. "*Tractatus Super Psalmum Vicesimum* of Richard Rolle of Hampole." Diss. Univ. of Illinois 1968.

Dolan finds this treatise interesting because of its mystical point of view, biographical information, and vigorous, polished style. His critical text is based on six manuscripts of the late 14th and early 15th centuries and one early printed edition. An English translation is appended.

Contra Amatores Mundi (*Liber de Amore Dei Contra Amatores Mundi*)

261. Theiner, Paul F., ed. *The Contra Amatores Mundi*. Berkeley and Los Angeles: University of California Press, 1968.

Theiner provides a good introduction on the content,

structure, and rhetorical devices of the work, a description of the manuscripts, a critical edition based on MS.
18932 of the John Rylands Library in Manchester, and an
English translation.

Incendium Amoris

262. Deanesly, Margaret, ed. *The Incendium Amoris of Richard
     Rolle of Hampole*. Manchester: The University Press;
     London and New York: Longmans, Green & Co., 1915; rpt.
     Folcroft, Pa.: Folcroft Library Edition, 1974.

     A critical edition of the long text of the *Incendium
     Amoris*, based on MS. Emmanuel College, Cambridge 35,
     with an introduction on the manuscript tradition and
     printed editions, subject matter of the *Incendium*, and
     its relation to Rolle's *Commentary on the Canticles*.

263. ————. "The *Incendium Amoris* of Richard Rolle and St.
     Bonaventure." *English Historical Review*, 29 (1914),
     98-101.

     This article traces the circumstances whereby Rolle's
     Incendium is erroneously attributed to Bonaventure,
     under its old title of *De Triplici Via*, and also suggests
     the Council of Constance as the link between the two
     works.

264. Heseltine, George C., trans. *The Fire of Love*. London:
     Burns, Oates & Washbourne, Ltd., 1935.

     A modern English translation of the *Incendium Amoris*,
     based on MS. Emmanuel College, Cambridge 35. (Note:
     Heseltine's translations of Chap. 20, "On Prayer," and
     Chap. 6, "On the True Knowledge of God," appear in *Ave
     Maria*, 37 [1933], 499; and 38 [1933], 755-6 respectively.)

265. Kelly, Henry Ansgar. *Love and Marriage in the Age of
     Chaucer*. Ithaca, N.Y.: Cornell Univ. Press, 1975,
     pp. 313-28.

     Kelly analyzes Richard Rolle's treatment of human and
     divine love in the *Incendium Amoris*.

266. Wolters, Clifton, ed. *The Fire of Love*. Harmondsworth,
     Middlesex, and Baltimore, Md.: Penguin Books, 1972.

     A modern English translation of the longer version of
     the *Incendium Amoris* in Margaret Deanesly's 1915 edition,
     preceded by an excellent introduction on Rolle, the

authenticity of his mysticism, and a brief excursis on
his alliterative style, his "Englishness," and his
genuine canon.

De Emendatione Vitae (*De Emendatione Peccatoris*)

267. Denis, Leopold, trans. *Du Péché à l'amour divin ou*
      l'amendment du pécheur. Paris: Declée, 1927.

      A French translation of the *De Emendatione*, with an
      introductory essay on Rolle's mysticism, showing simi-
      larities between Rolle and Richard of St. Victor, and
      notes on the text and sources.

Richard Misyn's Middle English Translations of the *De Emendatione Vitae* and *Incendium Amoris* into *The Mending of Life* (1434) and *The Fire of Love* (1435)

268. A.P., ed. *The Amending of Life.* London: Burns, Oates &
      Washbourne, Ltd., 1927.

      A slightly modernized edition of the Misyn translation,
      with an introduction.

269. Comper, Frances M.M., ed. *The Fire of Love or Melody of*
      Love and The Mending of Life or Rule of Living. Introd.
      Evelyn Underhill. London: Methuen & Co., Ltd., 1914;
      rpt. 1920.

      Ms. Underhill's introduction places Rolle in the broad
      spectrum of medieval mysticism. Ms. Comper's modern
      English edition of the Misyn translations is based on a
      collation of MSS. Corpus Christi College 236, B.L. Add.
      37790, and others. The two texts are preceded by a
      translation of the *Legenda* in the *Office of the Blessed*
      Hermit Richard, and there is an excellent selective
      bibliography.

270. Harford, Dundas, ed. *The Mending of Life.* London: H.R.
      Allenson, 1913.

      A modern English edition of Misyn's translation, drawn
      from MS. Cambridge Ff.v.40 (now first published), with
      an introduction on Rolle's mysticism and a discussion of
      why Anglicans pursue the study of Catholic mystics.

271. Harvey, Ralph, ed. *The Fire of Love and the Mending of*
      Life or The Rule of Living of Richard Rolle. EETS
      O.S. 106. London: Kegan Paul, Trench, Trübner, 1896;
      rpt. Kraus, 1973.

An edition of Richard Misyn's translation, drawn from
MS. Corpus Christi College, Oxford 336, with marginal
glosses in modern English.

272. Hubbard, H.L., ed. *The Amending of Life*. London: John
M. Watkins, 1922.

A modern English version of the Misyn translation.

273. Hulme, William H., ed. *Richard Rolle of Hampole's
Mending of Life from the Fifteenth Century Worcester
Cathedral MS. F. 172*. Cleveland: Western Reserve
Univ. Press, 1918.

An edition of the Middle English text, with an introduction giving an extensive account of the contents of
MS. F. 172, both works by Rolle and other mystical
writings, and stipulating that the translation is not
that of Richard Misyn.

274. Schnell, Eugen. *Die Traktate des Richard Rolle von
Hampole Incendium Amoris und Emendatio Vitae und
deren Übersetzung durch Richard Misyn*. Borna-Leipzig:
Universitätsverlag von R. Naske, 1932.

A painstaking investigation of Misyn's translations,
vis-à-vis the original works, and a discussion of
Rolle's Latin style.

275. Woods, Jerome P. "An Application of Paul Ricoeur's
Hermeneutic Phenomenology to the Symbols of Contem-
plative Union in Richard Rolle's *Fire of Love*." Diss.
DePaul Univ. 1977.

Rolle's primary symbols (heat, sweetness, and song)
are explored in their cosmic, oneiric, and poetic dimensions, using Ricoeur's structural concepts of Totality,
Self-Sufficiency, and Transparency as limit-ideas for
interpreting the symbols of union. The results are
synthesized in the concept of the "Unitive Will."
Ricoeur's "diagnostic" concept is then used to show the
relationships between primary symbols of union and the
traditional Christ-myths of redemptive wholeness in the
Fire of Love.

A2. ENGLISH PROSE WORKS: *English Psalter*; *Meditations on the
Passion* (H 1, pp. 83-103); The Short Prose Tracts of *The Bee
and the Stork* (H 1, p. 81), *Desire and Delight* (H 1, p. 197),
Ghostly Gladness (H 1, p. 81), *The Seven Gifts of the Holy
Ghost* (H 1, pp. 196-7), *Commentary on the Decalogue* (H 1,
pp. 195-6); and The Epistles *Ego Dormio* (H 1, pp. 50-61),
The Commandment (H 1, pp. 61-71), and *The Form of Living*
(H 1, pp. 1-50).

English Psalter

276.   Bramley, H.R., ed. *The Psalter or Psalms of David and
       Certain Canticles.* Oxford: Clarendon Press, 1884.

       An edition of Rolle's *English Psalter*, drawn pri-
       marily from MS. Univ. College, Oxford, 64.

277.   Callanan, Marion E. "An Edition of Richard Rolle's
       English Psalter with Notes and Commentary (Psalms 46-
       60." Diss. Fordham Univ. 1977.

       An edition based on MS. Univ. College, Oxford, 64,
       collated with seven other manuscripts used by Bramley,
       and nine additional manuscripts. Despite Middendorf's
       thesis that Rolle's work depends upon that of Peter
       Lombard, Callanan shows that Rolle adds much to further
       his own purpose of stirring the affections toward God,
       and also demonstrates that, despite a close relation-
       ship, the *English Psalter* is not a translation of the
       Latin.

278.   Cavallerano, Jerry D. "Richard Rolle's *English Psalter*,
       Psalms 31-45." Diss. Fordham Univ. 1976.

       According to Cavallerano, Rolle's personality is re-
       vealed through the tone and theme of the glosses, which
       are embellished with mystical characteristics. Despite
       Rolle's reliance on Peter Lombard, the tone of the
       language, mystical elements, and personal concerns re-
       flected in the glosses mark the work as uniquely Rolle's.

279.   Christ, Karl. "Zu Richard Rolle von Hampole, eine
       vatikanische Handschrift des *Psalmenkommentars.*"
       Archiv, 136 (1917), 35-9.

       Reports on a 15th-century Vatican manuscript of
       Rolle's *English Psalter*.

280. Collins, Marjorie O. "Psalms from the *English Psalter Commentary* of Richard Rolle." 2 vols. Diss. Univ. of Michigan 1966.

Vol. 1 contains an edition of 40 psalms from MS. Huntington 148, previously unpublished. Vol. 2 includes notes, a glossary, and an assessment of the work in the light of Rolle's own work and of the psalter commentary tradition from which it descended.

281. Everett, Dorothy. "The Middle English Prose *Psalter* of Richard Rolle of Hampole." *MLR*, 17 (1922), 217-27, 337-50; and 18 (1923), 381-93.

This seminal tripartite study deals with (1) manuscript relationships; (2) the connection between Rolle's version of the *Psalter* and earlier English versions, hypothesizing an indirect connection in terms of a common source which was an early Middle English (northern) interlinear gloss of the Vulgate; and (3) the purpose and history of the interpolated copies of the work, with a special emphasis on Lollard revisions.

282. Froomberg, Hilary. "The *English Psalter.*" *LS*, 2 (1948), 548-52.

Extracts from the *Psalter* (Prologue, Pss. 56 and 61), translated into modern English from the Thornton manuscript, with a note on Rolle's difficulty in combining colloquial and Latinate diction, and also regarding subsequent Lollard interpolations.

283. Hodgson, Geraldine. "Rolle and the Psalm of the Presence of God." *Laudate*, 4 (1926), 132-8.

A comparison of Rolle's treatment with that of Augustine.

284. ———. "Richard Rolle's Version of the Psalm *Cantate Domino.*" *Laudate*, 6 (1928), 27-30.

A close interpretative reading of the psalm.

285. ———, ed. *Richard Rolle's Version of the Penitential Psalms.* London: Faith Press, 1929.

An annotated modernization of Rolle's *Commentary* on the Penitential Psalms (Nos. 6, 31, 37, 50, 101, 129, and 142), which was written for Margaret Kirkeby and, according to Hodgson, should be read together with *The*

Form of Living. Hodgson's introduction also stresses
Rolle's relevance for today's world.

286. ————, ed. *Office Psalms from Rolle's Psalter and
      S. Augustine's Enarrationes.* London: Burns, Oates &
      Washbourne, 1932.

      A modern version of selected psalms, with an introduc-
      tion which discusses Rolle's indebtedness to both Peter
      the Lombard's *Catena* (*Commentarius Psalmas*) and Augustine's
      Enarrationes, which supports Maurice Noetinger's comments
      regarding Rolle's erudition and wide reading, questions
      the biographical veracity of the *Officium*, and opts for
      Rolle's priestly vocation.

287. Middendorf, Heinrich. *Studien zu Richard Rolle von
      Hampole unter besonderer Berücksichtigung seiner
      Psalmenkommentar.* Magdeburg: Priese und Fuhrman, 1888.

      A source study of Rolle's *English Psalter*, illustrating
      his heavy reliance on Peter the Lombard's *Catena*, and
      positing a similar reliance for the *Latin Psalter*.

288. Muir, Laurence. "A Comparison of the Rolle and Wyclif-
      fite Psalms with Those of the Authorized Version,
      together with a History of the Early *English Psalter*."
      Diss. Cornell Univ. 1934.

289. ————. "Influence of the Rolle and Wycliffite *Psalters*
      upon the *Psalter* of the Authorized Version." *MLR*, 30
      (1935), 302-10.

      A comparative study of the Rolle, Wycliffite, and
      Authorized Versions, which, allowing for linguistic
      development and changes in Scriptural translation and
      interpretation, clearly indicates an English tradition
      of translating the *Psalter*, extending from the Middle
      Ages onward, and, based on Dorothy Everett's findings,
      possibly from the Old English period.

290. Newton, Sandra S. "An Edition of Richard Rolle's *English
      Psalter*, the Prologue through Psalm 15." Diss. Fordham
      Univ. 1976.

      A definitive text of Rolle's *English Psalter*, based on
      the uninterpolated extant manuscripts. Establishes
      Peter the Lombard's *Catena* (*Commentarius Psalmas*) as
      Rolle's principal source, although Rolle did not slavishly
      copy nor totally rely on it. Analyzes Rolle's stylistic
      traits, which demonstrate his facility with English prose.

291. Paues, Anna. *A Fourteenth Century English Biblical Version.* Cambridge: Cambridge Univ. Press, 1902.

See the introduction of Paues's discussion of Lollard interpolations in Rolle's *English Psalter*, thereby refuting Forshall and Madden's statements in *The Wycliffite Versions of the Bible.*

Meditations on the Passion (Short version in MS. Cambridge Ll.I.8 and longer version in MSS. Cambridge Univ. Lib. Add. 3042, Bodl. e Musaeo 232, Uppsala Univ. C. 494, and B.L. Cotton Titus C. XIX)

292. Froomberg, Hilary. "The Virtue of Our Lord's Passion by Richard Rolle of Hampole." *LS*, 3 (1948), 221-5.

Modern English translation extracted from the *Meditations on the Passion*, with Froomberg commenting on possible Bernardian influence on Rolle's devotion to the Holy Name of Jesus.

293. Lindkvist, Harald, ed. "Richard Rolle's *Meditatio de Passione Domini.*" *Skrifter utgifna af Kungl. Humanistika Vetenskapa-Samfundet Uppsala*, 19 (1917), 1-72.

An edition of MS. Uppsala C. 494, collated with all other known copies, with an introduction, an important discussion of dialectical and linguistic features, and notes. An Uppsala fragment of the *Officium de S. Ricardo de Hampole* is contained in the Appendix, pp. 73-8.

294. Morgan, Margery M. "Versions of the *Meditations on the Passion* Ascribed to Richard Rolle." *MA*, 22 (1935), 339-43.

A study of the Anglo-Norman genesis and subsequent accretive Latin and English versions of this work, which suggests a "line of development likely to have been followed in the transmission and revision of other texts of a similar nature," and which casts doubt on the Rolle ascription.

295. Ullmann, J. "Studien zu Richard Rolle de Hampole I." *ES*, 7 (1884), 415-72.

An edition of Rolle's *Meditatio de Passione Domini* and the metrical homily *Speculum Vitae*, ascribed to William of Nassington, as contained in MS. Cambridge Ll. I. 8. Ullmann contends that Rolle authored both the *Speculum Vitae* and *Stimulus Conscientiae*. (See 660-7.)

296. Zupitza, J. "Zur *Meditacio Ricardi Heremite de Hampole
      de Passione Domini*" and "Zu dem Anfang des *Speculum
      Vitae*." *ES*, 12 (1889), 463-9.

      Comments on and offers emendations to Ullmann's
      readings contained in 295 above.

The Commandment

297. Amassian, Margaret. "An Edition of Richard Rolle's
      The Commandment." Diss. Fordham Univ. 1967.

      A critical edition drawn from MS. Cambridge Univ. Dd.
      V. 64 and other manuscripts. Amassian finds that *The
      Commandment*, written to a female religious in the begin-
      ning stages of spiritual development, has a fusion of
      subject matter and style not always achieved by Rolle,
      who here transmits the Augustinian spiritual tradition,
      emphasizing understanding, will, and memory as vital
      faculties in achieving union with God.

A3. LYRICS: Rolle's lyric corpus is difficult to define
     firmly. A large selection appears in Hl, pp. 71-82,
     363-74; and H 2, pp. 9-24. A more astute assessment of
     the canon in provided by Frances M.M. Comper, in Part II
     of her *The Life of Richard Rolle, Together with an
     Edition of his English Lyrics* (see 337), pp. 205-98,
     315-8, based on a study of the manuscripts and close
     links with Rolle's other works. Some helpful studies
     and anthologies follow.

298. Allen, Hope Emily. "The Mystical Lyrics of the *Manual
      des Pechiez*." *Romanic Review*, 9 (1918), 154-93.

      A discussion of the affinity of Anglo-Norman and
      Middle English literatures in general, and specifically,
      the religious and mystical lyrics, with the beginnings
      of the English mystical movement of the 14th century
      residing in the Anglo-Norman literature of the 13th.
      There is an especially valuable discussion of assessing
      the literature of England during the 12th and 13th cen-
      turies in terms of the collective literature written
      in English, Latin, and Anglo-Norman.

299. ————. "On Richard Rolle's Lyrics." *MLR*, 14 (1919),
      320-1.

      Ms. Allen points to translations of sections of Rolle's

Incendium Amoris, occurring in two Middle English mystical lyrics of the 14th century, illustrating the circulation in English of Rolle's Latin works. Allen also
cites other English translations of Rolle's Latin works,
such as those included in the *Poor Caitiff*, which illustrate the process of metamorphosis and transmutation of
texts that occurred with the circulation of devotional
and mystical writings in the Middle Ages.

300. Brown, Carleton F., ed. *Religious Lyrics of the XIVth
     Century*. Oxford: Clarendon Press, 1952.

     See introduction, p. xix, and lyrics from the "School
     of Richard Rolle," pp. 93-109, with notes on pp. 269-71.

301. ———, and Rossell Hope Robbins. *The Index of Middle
     English Verse*. New York: Columbia Univ. Press, 1943.

     Lyrics by or attributed to Rolle are "God þat es in
     mageste/ One God and persons thre" (980); "Ihesu my
     lefe Ihesu my loue: Ihesu my couetyne" (1733); "Luf es
     Lyf þat lastes ay" (2007); "My kynge þe watur grett/
     and þe blod he swett" (2250); "My sange es in syhtyng/
     my lufe es in langynge" (2270); "Qwen wil þu come &
     comforth me/ & bryng me out of kare" (4056). See also
     Supplement by Rossell Hope Robbins and John L. Cutler.
     Lexington: Univ. of Kentucky Press, 1965.

302. Davies, R.T., ed. *Medieval English Lyrics: A Critical
     Anthology*. London: Faber and Faber, Ltd., 1963;
     Evanston, Ill.: Northwestern Univ. Press, 1964, 1967,
     1969.

     "A song of love for Jesus," pp. 22, 38-9, 40, 108-10,
     322.

303. Dronke, Peter. "The Rise of the Religious Lyric." In
     The Medieval Lyric. London: Hutchinson Univ. Press,
     1968; 2nd ed. Cambridge and New York: Cambridge Univ.
     Press, 1977, pp. 52-85.

304. Gibinska, Marta. "Some Observations on the Themes and
     Techniques of the Medieval English Religious Love
     Lyric." *English Studies*, 57 (1976), 103-14.

     Poems from the "School of Richard Rolle" are among the
     lyrics considered in relation to the distinction between
     earthly and divine love, the use of secular patterns,
     the presence of love longing and desire for mystical

union with God (found to be especially characteristic
of the Rolle School), and the treatment of Christ's
Passion.

305. Gray, Douglas. *Themes and Images in the Medieval
      Religious Lyric*. London: Routledge and Kegan Paul,
      1972.

      An informative introduction to the lyric, pp. 3-58;
      "Jesu my joy and my lovynge," pp. 69-70, 79-80; and "I
      slepe and my hert wakes," pp. 159-60.

306. Hettich, Blaise. "A Critical Study of the Lyrics of
      Richard Rolle." Diss. Notre Dame Univ. 1957.

      Provides a rhetorical, structural, and thematic analy-
      sis of the lyrics edited by Hope Emily Allen in her
      English Writings of Richard Rolle (see 317), all of
      which concentrate on describing the intimate relationship
      between Christ and the soul. Hettich transcribes Rolle's
      Canticum Amoris, and compares "Luf es Lyf" to the cor-
      responding passages in the *Incendium Amoris*, contending
      that lyric preceded the treatise.

307. Knowlton, Mary A. *The Influence of Richard Rolle and
      of Julian of Norwich on the Middle English Lyric*.
      The Hague and Paris: Mouton Press, 1973.

      This study places Rolle squarely in the 14th-century
      meditational tradition, but does little to support the
      thesis of Rolle's direct influence on the lyric, and
      even less with regard to Julian.

308. Kuhn, Franz. *Über die Verfasserschaft der in Horstmanns
      Library of Early English Writers: Richard Rolle de
      Hampole anthaltenen lyrischen Gedichte*. Greifswald:
      Julius Abel, 1900.

      A careful study of Horstmann's ascription of lyrics
      to Rolle.

309. McGarry, Loretta. *The Holy Eucharist in Middle English
      Homiletic and Devotional Prose*. Washington, D.C.:
      Catholic Univ. of America, 1936.

      Includes a discussion of Rolle's "Hymn to Jesus Christ."

310. Manning, Stephen. *Wisdom and Number: Toward a Critical
      Appraisal of the Middle English Religious Lyric*.
      Lincoln: Univ. of Nebraska Press, 1962.

See Chap. 3, "Some Religious Structures," and pp. 56-9
for a discussion of "Luf es lyf þat lastes ay."

311. Rasin, Mary E. *Evidences of Romanticism in the Poetry
of Medieval England*. Louisville: Slater Co., 1929.

In her discussion of Rolle, Rasin contends that his
heartfelt response to the Passion of Christ made him a
leader of the "medieval romantic movement."

312. Robbins, Rossell Hope. "On the Mediaeval Religious
Lyric." Diss. Cambridge Univ. 1937.

313. Rogers, William E. *Image and Abstraction: Six Middle
English Religious Lyrics*. Copenhagen: Rosenkilde
and Bagger, 1972.

See especially Chap. V, "Rolle's 'Jhesu, God Sonn,'"
pp. 69-81.

314. Sisam, Kenneth. *Fourteenth Century Verse and Prose*.
Oxford: Clarendon Press, 1921.

"Love Is Life," pp. 37-40, 214.

315. Wilson, Sarah. "The Longleat Version of 'Love Is Life.'"
RES, N.S. 10 (1959), 337-46.

A careful assessment of this poem as it appears in
different manuscripts and editions, arguing that MS.
Longleat 29 is correct in its presentation of the poem
as three separate pieces, and affords some superior
readings over the versions contained in MSS. Cambridge
Univ. Dd.5.64, III and Lambeth 853.

316. Woolf, Rosemary. "Richard Rolle and the Mystical
School." In *The Religious Lyric in the Middle Ages*.
Oxford: Clarendon Press, 1968, pp. 159-79.

B. ANTHOLOGIES OF ROLLE'S LATIN AND ENGLISH WORKS

The paramount Rolle anthology is Carl Horstmann's seminal *Yorkshire Writers: Richard Rolle
of Hampole ... and His Followers* (see 107).
While some of his introductory comments in
Vols. 1 and 2 and his proposed canon of genuine
works are to be questioned, he has many perceptive

and informative insights, and provides an
invaluable collocation of Rolle's texts.

317. Allen, Hope Emily, ed. *English Writings of Richard
      Rolle, Hermit of Hampole.* Oxford: Clarendon Press,
      1931, rpt. 1963; and St. Clair Shores, Mich.:
      Scholarly Press, 1971.

      A shorter study of Rolle, drawing on the author's
      MLA monograph and intended for students of literary and
      religious history, with glossary and notes to assist
      the general and scholarly reader. In addition to a
      lucid introduction about Rolle's life and his importance
      as a mystic, and a critical assessment of his canon,
      Allen provides Middle English selections or full texts
      of the following: *English Psalter* (Prologue and Pss. 3,
      12, 56, and 61-2); *Meditations on the Passion*, Texts I
      and II; eight lyrics; *The Bee and the Stork* and *Desire
      and Delight*; and the epistles *Ego Dormio, The Command-
      ment*, and *The Form of Living*.

318. de la Bigne, Marguerin, ed. *Maxima Bibliotheca Veterum
      Patrum, et Antiquorum Scriptorum Ecclesiasticorum.*
      Lyons, 1677.

      Vol. 26 contains several of Rolle's Latin works, in-
      cluding the *Emendatio Vitae*.

319. Faber, F., ed. *D. Richardi Pampolitani Anglosaxonis
      Eremitae, Viri in divinis scripturis ac veteri illa
      solidaque Theologia eruditissmi, in Psalterium
      Davidicum atque alia quaedem sacrae scripturae
      monumenta (quae versa indicabit pagella) compendiosa
      iuxtaque pia Enarratio.* Coloniae: ex officina
      Melchioris Nouesiani, 1536.

      Contains *In Psalterium Davidicum Enarratio, In Aliquot
      Capitula Job, In Threnos, In Psalmum XX, Emendatio Vitae,
      Nominis Jesu Encomium Celeberrimum, In Orationem
      Dominicam, In Symbolum Apostolicum*, among other works.

320. Harrell, John C. *Selected Writings of Richard Rolle.*
      London: SPCK, 1963.

      A biographical introduction and modern English selec-
      tions from Rolle's shorter treatises and meditations,
      including *Desire and Delight, The Seven Gifts of the
      Holy Ghost*, and *Meditations on the Passion*.

321. Heseltine, George C. *Selected Works of Richard Rolle*.
London: Longmans, Green and Co., 1930.

The introduction consists in an enthusiastic encomium
to Rolle as the greatest of English mystics who reached
"the highest pinnacle of prayer," and as the Father of
English Prose, who took the doctorate at the University
of Paris--all controversial statements. The remainder
of the work contains modernized translations of the
majority of Rolle's English works.

322. Hodgson, Geraldine, ed. *The Form of Perfect Living and
Other Prose Treatises of Richard Rolle of Hampole*.
London: Thomas Baker, 1910.

In addition to the *Form of Living* and other tracts,
Hodgson includes *On Daily Work*, which is considered a
doubtful work (see 329).

323. ————. *Some Minor Works of Richard Rolle with the
Privity of the Passion by S. Bonaventura*. London:
John M. Watkins, 1923.

Rolle's works include *Ego Dormio, The Commandment*,
and *The Gifts of the Holy Ghost*. Also included is *The
Mirror of St. Edmund*, which Hodgson considers a "storehouse" of Rolle's subjects and ideas.

324. Noetinger, Maurice, ed. *Le Feu d'Amour, le Modèle de
la Vie parfait, Le Pater par Richard Rolle l'Ermite
de Hampole*. Tours: Maison Alfred Mame et Fils, 1928.

A French translation of the Latin *Incendium Amoris,
De Emendatio Vitae*, and *Super Orationem Dominicam*,
together with Noetinger's excellent commentary on the
works and their sources.

325. Perry, George G., ed. *English Prose Treatises of
Richard Rolle de Hampole*. EETS O.S. 20. London:
Oxford Press, 1866, rev. 1921 (for 1920); rpt. Kraus,
1973.

Contains twelve prose selections from the Thornton
manuscript, several of which are erroneously attributed
to Rolle, such as the *Anhede of Godd with Mannes Soule
(Of Angels' Song)*, now ascribed to Walter Hilton.

C. SPURIOUS OR DOUBTFUL WORKS

326. Aarts, Florent Gerard. *The Pater Noster of Richard
      Ermyte. A Late Middle English Exposition of the Lord's
      Prayer.* Nijmegen: Janssen, 1967.

      An edition, based on Westminster School MS. 3, with
      variants, notes, and glossary. The introduction contains
      thorough comments on the text, and a valuable survey of
      the significance of the Pater Noster commentaries for
      medieval devotional and mystical literature. Aarts
      adopts Hope Emily Allen's arguments against Rolle's
      authorship, but admits the question demands a great deal
      of additional study.

327. Adler, Max, and M. Kaluza. "Über die Richard Rolle de
      Hampole: Zugeschrieben Paraphrase der sieben Buss-
      psalmen." *ES*, 10 (1887), 215-55.

      An exploration for the identity of the author, whether
      Richard Rolle or Richard Maidestone, and a critical
      edition of the text. (See 285.) For another Psalter
      possibly ascribable to Rolle, see H 2, pp. 129-273.

328. Arntz, Mary L. "Þe *Holy Boke Gratia Dei*: An Edition
      with Commentary." Diss. Fordham Univ. 1961.

      An edition of a previously unedited late 14th-century
      composition, attributed to Richard Rolle. Arntz offers
      substantial proof against Rolle's authorship.

329. Hodgson, Geraldine, ed. *Rolle and "Our Daily Work."*
      London: The Faith Press, 1929.

      An edition of *"Our Daily Work*, drawn from MSS. Arundel
      507 and Thornton, with an excellent introduction on
      "Asceticism and Mysticism," stressing Rolle's ascetic
      commitment (pp. 1-24), and a strong claim for Rolle's
      authorship of the treatise (pp. 101-17), which upholds
      Horstmann's contention, and disputes Hope Emily Allen's
      rejection of the treatise from Rolle's canon. (Note:
      Text in H 1, pp. 137-56, 310-21).

330. Wormald, Francis. "*De Passione Secundum Ricardum*
      (Possibly a New Work by Richard Rolle)." *Laudate*, 13
      (1935), 37-48.

      A brief analysis and the text of a heretofore unreported
      meditation ascribed to Rolle, and contained in MS. Cotton
      Titus C. 19 of the late 15th century.

D. BIOGRAPHICAL STUDIES

The two main sources of biographical information are an *Officium* and *Miracula*, written
toward the end of the 14th century by someone
attached to Hampole Priory to promote Rolle's
canonization, and biographical references in
his works. As the following studies attest,
there is disagreement over his birthplace,
his reasons for leaving Oxford, his possible
attendance at the Sorbonne, his attitudes
toward ecclesiastical authority, his status
(priest or layman), and other considerations.
In addition to the items in this section, see
also 258-60 and 269.

331. Allen, Hope Emily. "The Birthplace of Richard Rolle."
TLS, 30 (1931), 683.

Upholds Thornton as Rolle's birthplace.

332. ⸻. "Richard Rolle." *TLS*, 31 (1932), 516.

Maintains the theory that Rolle was a layman and not
a priest, as proposed by Dom Maurice Noetinger.

333. Arnould, Emile J. "Richard Rolle and a Bishop: A
Vindication." *Bulletin of the John Rylands Library*,
21 (1937), 55-77.

Reviews and disagrees with Horstmann's and Hope Emily
Allen's interpretation of the passage in the *Melos
Amoris* concerning Rolle's challenge to the bishop.
According to Arnould, the picture of Rolle as an ec-
clesiastical outlaw, reformer, and "potential schismatic"
contradicts his usual regard for authority and orthodoxy.

334. ⸻. "On Richard Rolle's Patrons: A New Reading."
MA, 6 (1937), 122-4.

Because of the words *ad scolas* which appear in two
manuscripts of Rolle's *De Amore Dei Contra Amatores
Mundi*, Arnould conjectures that the woman referred to
is the wife of the squire John de Dalton, which supports
Horstmann's conjecture. Arnould admits, however, that
there are other possibilities.

335. ⸻. "Richard Rolle and the Sorbonne." *Bulletin of
the John Rylands Library*, 23 (1939), 68-101.

Examines four manuscripts relating to the history of

the Sorbonne from the Arsenal Library (MSS. 1020, 1021,
1022, and 1228), and concludes that any assertion that
Rolle sojourned at the Sorbonne is unwarranted.

336. ———. "Richard Rolle of Hampole." *Month*, N.S. 23
        (1960), 13-25.

        A clear explanation of Rolle's canon, especially his
        more contemplative writings--*De Emendatione Vitae*,
        Form of Living, and *Melos Amoris*--as they reveal Rolle's
        life and spiritual progress. Also commends Rolle's
        prose style, citing R.W. Chambers.

337. Comper, Frances M.M. *The Life of Richard Rolle, Together
        with an Edition of his English Lyrics*. London and
        Toronto: J.M. Dent & Sons, Ltd., 1928; rpt. New York:
        Barnes and Noble, 1969.

        A full account of Rolle's life in the 14th-century
        milieux of Oxford and Yorkshire, maintaining his "dis-
        like of theological subtleties" and of ecclesiastical
        authority, and assessing his mysticism, his works, and
        the sources thereof. Following her appraisal of Rolle's
        lyrics in Part II, there is an appendix, giving a trans-
        lation of the *Legenda* in the *Officium*.

338. Hardwick, J.C. "A Medieval Anti-Scholastic." *Modern
        Churchman*, 6 (1916-17), 251-5.

        A discussion of Rolle's aversion to scholasticism,
        thereby supporting Horstmann's and Comper's view.

339. Heseltine, George C. *Great Yorkshiremen*. London:
        Longmans, Green and Co., 1932.

        Chap. 7 extols Rolle as "the father of English prose,
        a fiery poet, and a saint," and warns against psycho-
        logical or pseudoscientific attempts to explain the
        spiritual life, which resides in the realm of revelation
        and inspiration.

340. ———. "Richard Rolle." *TLS*, 31 (1932), 271.

        A discussion of Rolle's status as a layman or cleric.

341. ———. "Richard Rolle: 1349-1949; A Master of Medieval
        English." *Tablet*, 194 (1949), 214-5.

        A commemoration of the sixth centenary of Rolle's
        death, with a discussion of his works and contribution
        to English prose.

342.   Hodgson, Geraldine.   "Concerning Richard Rolle."   *CQR*,
       108 (1929), 224-37.

       A discussion of three controversial points in the
       Officium (Rolle's first patron, the authenticity and
       authorship of the *Officium*, and the moment when he be-
       came a hermit), as handled by Frances Comper, Maurice
       Noetinger, and Hope Emily Allen.

343.   James, S.B.   "Medieval Individualist."   *NCW*, 169 (1949),
       440-5.

       Influenced by Frances Comper and others, James has
       written an impressionistic biography, attributing to
       Rolle a "robust independence" in his rejection of higher
       learning, religious vocation, and monastic life style.

344.   Jeffery, Reginald W.   "The Hermits of Thornton: Richard
       Rolle and William of Dalby."   In *Thornton-le-Dale:
       Being the History of the People of Thornton-le-Dale*.
       Wakefield: The West Yorkshire Printing Co., 1931, pp.
       23-40.

       Vigorously maintains that Rolle was not born in
       Thornton-le-Dale.

345.   Lawley, Stephen W., ed.   *York Breviary 2*, cols. 785-820.
       Surtees Society, 1889.

       See Appendix V for the Latin text of the *Officium* and
       Miracula, taken from the incomplete text in MS. Lincoln
       C.5.2, with lacunae supplied from MS. B.L. Cotton Tib.
       A. XV.

346.   Meadows, George D.   "The Father of English Mysticism:
       Richard Rolle of Hampole, 1290-1349."   *NCW*, 126 (1928),
       456-60.

       An attempt to assess Richard Rolle less as a young
       mystical prodigy and more as a likeable human being,
       highly educated, drawn to the eremitic life, and cen-
       tering his spiritual life around love.

347.   Moorman, F.W.   "Richard Rolle, the Yorkshire Mystic."
       Transactions of the Yorkshire Dialect Society, 3, Pt.
       16 (1914), 89-106.

       A chauvinistic account of Rolle's life and works,
       in the light of his Yorkshire origins.

348. Noetinger, Maurice. "The Biography of Richard Rolle."
      Month, 147 (1926), 22-30.

      In an effort to evolve the "real" Richard Rolle,
      Noetinger examines the *Officium*, *Miracula*, and autobio-
      graphical references in his writings. He coalesces
      some of the discrepancies between these sources by up-
      holding Rolle's having secured a Doctor of Divinity at
      the Sorbonne.

349. Patch, Howard R. "Richard Rolle, Hermit and Mystic."
      American Church Monthly, 28 (1928), 32-8, 108-14.

      A sympathetic treatment of Rolle's life and mysticism.

350. Pepler, Conrad. "English Spiritual Writers III. Richard
      Rolle." *CR*, 44 (1959), 78-89.

      A restrained, objective assessment of Rolle's mysticism,
      with references to Julian of Norwich.

351. Underhill, Evelyn. "Ricardus Heremita." *Dublin Review*,
      183 (1926), 176-87.

      An excellent summary of Hope Emily Allen's findings
      in *Writings Ascribed to Richard Rolle, Hermit of Hampole,
      and Materials for His Biography* (see 359), pointing out
      Rolle's "inner history and status as a mystic."

352. Watts, H.G. "Richard Rolle of Hampole." *NCW*, 103
      (1916), 798-804.

      A treatment of Rolle's life and mysticism, which,
      according to Watts, resides in a consuming love of God,
      as it does with Catholic mystics through the ages.

353. Whiting, Charles Edwin. "Richard Rolle of Hampole."
      Yorkshire Archaeological Society Journal, 37 (1951),
      5-23.

      Praises Rolle as the greatest of English mystics, and
      explores in detail his life (Whiting supports his
      training at the Sorbonne) and his writings.

354. Woolley, Reginald M., ed. *The Officium and the Miracula
      of Richard Rolle of Hampole*. London: SPCK; New York:
      The Macmillan Co., 1919.

      Complete text, drawn from the three extant manuscripts:
      Bodl. e Musaeo 193, Lincoln C.5.2, and B.L. Cotton Tib.
      A. XV, with a brief introduction. (See also 258-60, 269).

E. GENERAL CRITICAL STUDIES

355. Alford, John A. "Biblical *Imitatio* in the Writings of
     Richard Rolle." *ELH*, 40 (1973), 1-23.

     Argues that Rolle's prose style reflects the medieval
     rhetorical strategy of biblical *imitatio*, and concludes
     with the suggestion of the need for further research
     on Rolle's style.

356. ———. "The Biblical Identity of Richard Rolle."
     FCEMN, 2/4 (1976), 21-5.

     Alford shows that the nature of medieval autobiography
     must be studied in order to understand Rolle's telling
     of his life story, especially in view of its Christo-
     logical parallels.

357. Allen, Hope Emily. *The Authorship of the Prick of
     Conscience*. Radcliffe College Monographs, 15. Boston
     and New York: Ginn and Co., 1910.

     Presents an exhaustive study of Rolle's manuscripts,
     and definitely disproves Rolle's authorship of the
     Prick, an opinion which has achieved scholarly consensus.

358. ———. "The *Speculum Vitae*: Addendum." *PMLA*, 32 (1917),
     133-62.

     A discussion which disavows Rolle's authorship of the
     Speculum Vitae and explores other putative sources of
     the work. (See 660-7.)

359. ———. *Writings Ascribed to Richard Rolle, Hermit of
     Hampole, and Material for His Biography*. MLA Monograph
     Series 3. New York: D.C. Heath and Co.; London: Oxford
     Univ. Press, 1927.

     Definitive early study of Rolle's authentic and
     ascribed canon of works, the manuscript tradition, his
     biography, and an assessment of Rolle's place in English
     religious and literary history. Also contains a list of
     publications relating to Rolle, up to 1927. Ms. Allen
     has been criticized for her inadequate understanding of
     medieval religion and for some of her more conjectural
     conclusions, but the book remains a landmark in Rolle
     studies. See Dorothy Everett's favorable review in *RES*,
     5 (1929), 79-84, citing Allen's substantial contribution
     to Rolle scholarship, but pointing to the weakness of

her arguments regarding Rolle's lyrics. Also see
Howard Patch's generally complimentary review in
Speculum, 4 (1929), 469-71.

360. ————. "New Manuscripts of Richard Rolle." *TLS*, 31
(1932), 202.

A report on two newly found manuscripts: Bodl. Douce
C. 13, containing Rolle's *Super Orationem Dominicam* and
lyrics of the Rolle "school"; and Bodl. Lat. th. d. 15,
written by Robert Parkin, which is the only volume that
can be traced to the Hampole district.

361. Amassian, Margaret G. "The Rolle Material in Bradfer-
Lawrence MS. 10 and Its Relationships to Other Rolle
Manuscripts." *Manuscripta*, 23 (1979), 67-78.

A careful study of the unique fragment of an English
translation of Rolle's *Emendatio Vitae*, which introduced
the text of *The Commandment* in MS. 10. This fragment
is the sole witness to a lost translation of the
Emendatio. Amassian also establishes that all seven
complete translations of the *Emendatio* derive from the
Latin tradition and not each other.

362. Bridgett, T.E. "Richard Rolle, the Hermit." *Dublin
Review*, 121 (1897), 284-93.

An analysis of Horstmann's findings on Rolle.

363. Elwin, Verier. *Richard Rolle, A Christian Sannyāsē*.
The Bhaktas of the World, No. 3. Madras: Christian
Literature Society for India, 1930.

An interesting comparison of Rolle's teaching on contemplation, his life, and his works with Hindu contemplative doctrine and poetics.

364. Gilmour, J. "Notes on the Vocabulary of Richard Rolle."
N&Q, 201 (1956), 94-5.

Points to the uneven representation of Rolle's vocabulary in the *OED*, and cites early recordings from Rolle's
works which antedate the *OED* entries.

365. Hahn, Arnold. *Quellenuntersuchungen zu Richard Rolles
englischen Schriften*. Halle: Vereinigten Friedricks-
Universität Halle-Wittenberg, 1900.

A study of sources for the English epistles and other
works attributed to Rolle, including the *Prick of Con-
science*.

366. Henningsen, G.H. *Über die Wortstellung in den Prosa-schriften Richard Rolles von Hampole*. Erlangen: Junge und Sohn, 1911.

367. Hodgson, Geraldine. *The Sanity of Mysticism. A Study of Richard Rolle*. London: Faith Press Ltd., 1926; rpt. Folcroft, Pa.: Folcroft Library Editions, 1977.

     A defense of mysticism against its critics, based on a survey of the life, background, and works of Rolle. Includes excerpts from the writings of Rolle and his contemporaries. Cites Thomas de Hales's "Love Rune" as perhaps the most mystical composition in Middle English before Rolle, and also *Elene* as an example of "tentative mystical gleams in Anglo-Saxon literature."

368. James, S.B. "Richard Rolle, Englishman." *CR*, N.S. 20 (1941), 31-44.

     Depicts Rolle as the embodiment of the essential English spirit and spirituality, in his use of the vernacular, independent and roving life style, nonconformism, common sense and moderation, passion and rationality.

369. Jennings, Margaret. "Richard Rolle and the Three Degrees of Love." *DR*, 93 (1975), 193-200.

     In an astute analysis of Rolle's *Commandment*, *Form of Living*, and *Emendatio Vitae*, Jennings compares his three degrees of love with accounts of mystical experiences in Francis of Assisi, Bernard of Clairvaux, the Victorines, and his own *Ego Dormio*. She sees in Rolle no description of truly unitive experiences to match those in Dame Julian or the *Cloud*.

370. Lehmann, Max. *Untersuchungen zur mystischen Terminologie Richard Rolles*. Jena: Gustav Neuenhohn, 1936.

     An exploration of specific Middle English and Latin terms as they appear in Rolle's canon. Lehmann's excursus on *calor*, *dulcor*, and *canor*, pp. 25-59, is especially enlightening.

371. Madigan, Mary F. *The Passio Domini Theme in the Works of Richard Rolle: His Personal Contribution in its Religious, Cultural, and Literary Context*. Elizabethan and Renaissance Studies, No. 79. Salzburg, 1978.

     A study of Rolle's *Meditations on the Passion*, including the manuscript tradition, a close stylistic analysis, and

a convincing argument for Rolle's authorship (Appendix
C), along with an excellent introduction on Rolle's
milieu, an assessment of the *Passio Domini* theme in
Rolle's other works, and a consideration of Rolle's
contribution to medieval devotional literature and to
the development of Middle English literary prose.
Appendix B is a transcription of the longer version of
the *Meditations on the Passion* contained in MS. B.L.
Cotton Titus C. XIX, heretofore unprinted. There is
also an extensive bibliography on Rolle. Reviewed by
Valerie Lagorio in *Speculum*, 55 (1980), 409-10, and
Dennis Rygiel, *FCEMN*, 6/2 (1980), 91-4.

372. Niederstenbruch, Alex. "Die geistige Haltung Richard
      Rolles." *Archiv*, 175 (1939), 50-64.

      A careful analysis of Rolle's mysticism in its 14th-
      century context.

373. O'Domhnaill, Padraich A. "A Critical Study with Diplo-
      matic Texts of Revised and Expanded Versions of
      English Works of Rolle in MS. T.C.D. C. 5. 7 (155):
      with an Analysis of Rolle's Teaching against the Back-
      ground of Traditional Spirituality." Diss. Univ.
      College, Dublin 1959.

374. Olmes, Antonie. "Sprache und Stil der englischen Mystik
      des Mittelalters, unter besonderer Berücksichtigung
      des Richard Rolle von Hampole." *Studien zur englischen
      Philologie*, 76 (1933), 1-100.

      Though outdated in some respects, this study illustrates
      Rolle's use of rhetorical devices and metaphorical pat-
      terns in his English and Latin works, and analyzes
      Rolle's prose and his mystical style.

375. Patch, Howard R. "Richard Rolle, Hermit and Mystic."
      American Church Monthly, 38 (1930), 32-8, 108-14.

376. Pepler, Conrad. "Love of the Word." *LS*, 2 (1948),
      540-6.

      A moving analysis of the *Quia Amore Langueo* theme in
      Rolle's works, concluding that Rolle did not achieve the
      full degree of union with God experienced by the *Cloud*
      author, Julian, and John of the Cross.

377. Pulsford, Daniel B. "The Passion and the Poets: Richard
      Rolle." *Sign*, 15 (1938), 215-6.

Posits the centrality of the Christ Crucified theme to the poetry of Rolle and the writings of other 14th-century mystics, as well as its resurgence in the 18th century.

378. Relihan, Robert. "Richard Rolle and the Tradition of Thirteenth Century Devotional Literature." *FCEMN*, 4/4 (1978), 10-6.

An exploration of the informing influence of 13th-century devotional literature on the logic and form used by Rolle to express his own mystical beliefs. Special attention is given to Edmund of Abingdon's *Mirror* (*Speculum Ecclesiae* or *Religiosorum*), the *Ancrene Riwle*, and *Les Peines de Purgatorie*.

379. Renaudin, Paul. "Le Dénouement de l'amour dans la vie de Richard Rolle." *VS*, 61 (1938), 143-62.

A discussion of the terms *calor* and *dulcor* in Rolle's mystical writings.

380. ———. "Richard Rolle, poète de l'amour divin." *VS*, 62 (1940), 65-80.

A study of the significance of the term *canor* in Rolle's writings and mystical life.

381. Russell, Kenneth C. "Reading Richard Rolle." *Spirituality Today*, 30 (1978), 153-63.

An apologia for Rolle as an "authentic contemplative," based on a guide to the reading of *The Fire of Love*. Russell also includes a discussion on Rolle's view of friendship, his denunciation of false mystics, and, though a "maverick mystical hermit," his relevance to the modern world.

382. Rygiel, Dennis. "Structures and Style in Rolle's *The Form of Living.*" *FCEMN*, 4/1 (1978), 6-15.

Studies the interrelationships of chapters in *The Form of Living* and the ways in which individual chapters are organized. Argues that, contrary to the suggestions of some critics, the work's structure includes patterns other than repetition, citing classification and division as examples. This study points the way for similar analyses of Rolle's texts and other mystical writings.

383. Schneider, John P. *The Prose Style of Richard Rolle of Hampole, with Special Reference to its Euphuistic*

Tendencies. Baltimore, Md.: J.H. Furst, 1906.

With a focus of intellectual problems in the history
of English prose, Schneider analyzes Rolle's rhetorical
devices in some of his English works, and catalogs his
use of alliteration, as well as types of comparison and
contrast.

384. Schulte, Franz. "Das musikalische Element in der
      Mystik Richard Rolles von Hampole." Diss. Univ. of
      Bonn 1951.

385. Underhill, Evelyn. "Ricardus Heremita." *Dublin Review*,
      183 (1928), 176-87.

A treatment of Rolle's life, works, and influence,
drawn, in part, from assessments of the studies by Hope
Emily Allen, Margaret Deanesly, and R.M. Woolley, among
others.

386. Womack, Sam J., Jr. "The *Jubilus* Theme in the Later
      Writings of Richard Rolle." Diss. Duke University
      1961.

Appraises the mystical attainments of Richard Rolle
through studying his later works to see if the theme of
joy persists in them. Womack sees Rolle as using song
as the major symbol of mystical union.

387. Wright, Gilbert G. "The Definition of Love in Richard
      Rolle of Hampole." Diss. Univ. of Wisconsin 1963.

Analyzes Rolle's theory of love, which was an opera-
tion of the entire soul, including memory and intellect,
not just of the will alone. Wright also explores the
place of love in Rolle's teaching on prayer, contemplation, and union.

III. THE *CLOUD* AUTHOR

The anonymous author of *The Cloud of Unknowing* and its cognate tracts is an experienced spiritual director who alone among the English mystics espoused the apophatic tradition (*via negativa*) of mysticism. It is believed that he wrote his works in the latter part of the 14th century, after Richard Rolle and contemporary with or after Walter Hilton.

The *Cloud* author's canon consists of the following works: *The Cloud of Unknowing*; *The Book of Privy Counseling*; *Deonise Hid Diuinite*; *A Treatise of the Study of Wisdom That Is Called Benjamin* (H 1, pp. 162-72); *An Epistle of Prayer*; *An Epistle of Discretion of Stirrings*; *A Treatise of Discretion of Spirits*.

The *Cloud* author and his works are considered as follows:
A. Editions and Translations.
B. Critical Studies of the Identity of the *Cloud* Author.
C. Critical Studies of the Works.

A. EDITIONS AND TRANSLATIONS

388. *The Cloud of Unknowing. A Version in Modern English of a Fourteenth Century Classic*. 1st ed. New York: Pub. in assn. with Pendle Hill by Harper, 1948.

An abridged and rearranged version.

389. Collins, Henry, ed. *The Divine Cloud, with Notes and a Preface by Father Augustin Baker*. London: Thomas Richardson and Sons; and New York: Henry H. Richardson, 1871.

390.   Garrison, Anne. "The *Benjamin Minor* or the Preparation
       of the Mind for Contemplation by Richard of St. Vic-
       tor." Diss. Michigan State Univ. 1957.

391.   Grady, Sr. Laureen. "*A Pistle of Discrecioun of
       Stirings, or a Letter About How to Read One's Interior
       Aspirations.*" *Contemplative Review*, 10 (1977), 9-19.

       This Modern English translation is based on Phyllis
       Hodgson's critical edition, and was undertaken by Sr.
       Laureen "to make more widely available what belongs to
       the common patrimony of the whole mystical tradition."

392.   Guerne, Armel, ed. *Le nuage d'inconnaissance.* Paris:
       Éditions du Cahiers du Sud, 1953.

       A Modern French translation of the *Cloud*, with a very
       brief introduction.

393.   Hodgson, Phyllis, ed. *The Cloud of Unknowing and the
       Book of Privy Counselling.* EETS O.S. 218, 1944; rpt.
       London: Oxford Univ. Press, 1973.

       The critical edition, using MS. B.L. Harl. 674 as the
       base text. Hodgson's comprehensive introduction reviews
       the manuscript tradition, phonology and grammar, the
       subject matter and sources of the treatises, and the
       unresolved question of authorship. The reprinted edi-
       tion makes some slight corrections, adds some biblio-
       graphic entries, and slightly revises the glossary.

394.   ———, ed. *Deonise Hid Diuinite and Other Treatises
       Related to The Cloud of Unknowing.* EETS O.S. 231,
       1955; rpt. London: Geoffrey Cumberlege, 1958.

       The critical edition, using MS. B.L. Harl. 674 as the
       base text, of five treatises attributed to the author
       of the *Cloud* and *The Book of Privy Counselling*: *Deonise
       Hid Diuinite, A Tretyse of the Stodye of Wysdome that
       Men Clepen Beniamyn, A Pistle of Preier, A Pistle of
       Discrecioun of Stirings,* and *A Tretis of Discrescyon
       of Spirites.* In addition to an extensive introduction,
       which discusses the manuscripts, subject matter, style,
       and authorship, Hodgson presents the Latin sources of
       Deonise Hid Diuinite in Appendix A, and a critical edi-
       tion of *A Ladder of Foure Ronges by the which Men Mowe
       Wele Clyme to Heven* in Appendix B.

395.   Johnston, William, ed. *The Cloud of Unknowing and The
       Book of Privy Counseling.* Garden City, N.Y.: Image
       Books, 1973.

A Modern English edition of these two works, with an excellent introduction.

396. "A Letter on Prayer." *Way*, 7 (1967), 156-62.

Modern English versions of *An Epistle of Discretion of Stirrings* and *A Treatise of Discretion of Spirits*.

397. Llewelyn, Robert, ed. *The Epistle of Privy Counsel*. Norwich: Julian Shrine Publications, 1978.

An extract of the *Epistle* in Modern English.

398. McCann, Justin, ed. *The Cloud of Unknowing, and Other Treatises, by an English Mystic of the Fourteenth Century, with a Commentary on the Cloud by Augustine Baker*. London and New York, 1924; London, 1941, 1943, 1947, 1960; Springfield, Ill.: Templegate, 1964.

A popular modernized version by a noted scholar of the mystics.

399. Noetinger, Maurice, ed. *Le Nuage de l'inconnaissance et les épîtres qui s'y rattachent, par un anonyme anglais du quatorzième siècle*. Paris: Maison A. Muse, 1925.

An excellent French translation of the *Cloud* and its cognate tracts, which has been reprinted by the Abbey of Solesmes.

400. Okuda, Heihachiro, ed. *The Cloud of Unknowing*. Classic Library. Tokyo: Gendaischicho-sha, 1977.

A translation of the *Cloud* into Japanese, with 13 pages of introduction, 200 pages of text, and 18 pages of commentary.

401. Progoff, Ira, ed. *The Cloud of Unknowing*. New York, 1957; London, 1959; rpt. New York: Dell Publishing Co., Inc., 1973.

A very readable translation with an excellent introduction. Progoff approaches the *Cloud* as a source of information and insight which is helpful to modern psychology. He also sees the work as "a particularly sensitive, realistic, and objective description of the experimental work of the inner life."

401a. Riehle, Wolfgang, ed. *Die Wolke des Nichtwissens*. Einsiedeln: Johannes Verlag, 1980.

A German translation of the *Cloud*, with a sound introduction.

402.   Strakosch, Elizabeth, ed. *Die Wolke des Nichtwissens.*
        Einsiedeln: Johannes Verlag, 1958.

        A German translation of the *Cloud.*

403.   Underhill, Evelyn, ed. *A Book of Contemplation, the*
        Which is Called The Cloud of Unknowing, in the Which
        a Soul is Oned with God. London, 1912, 1922, 1934,
        1946, 1950; London: J.M. Watkins, 1970.

        A Modern English version, based on MS. B.L. Harl. 674,
        with an introduction.

404.   Walsh, James, ed. *A Letter of Private Direction. By the*
        Author of The Cloud of Unknowing. London: Burns &
        Oates, 1963.

        The Book of Privy Counseling, translated into modernized
        English, with a useful introduction.

405.   Wolters, Clifton, ed. *The Cloud of Unknowing.* Harmonds-
        worth, Middlesex; and Baltimore: Penguin Books, 1961,
        with many subsequent printings.

406.   ————. *The Cloud of Unknowing and Other Works.* Har-
        mondsworth, Middlesex: Penguin Books, 1978.

        Included in this reprint are the *Cloud*, *Epistle of*
        Privy Counsel, *Dionysius's Mystical Theology*, and
        Epistle of Prayer.

407.   ————. *A Study of Wisdom.* Fairacres Publication 75.
        Oxford: SLG Press, 1980.

        A modern version of the three *Cloud* author tracts which
        were not included in the 1978 Penguin edition (406):
        Benjamin Minor, *Discernment of Stirrings*, and *Discerning*
        of Spirits.

B. CRITICAL STUDIES OF
THE *CLOUD* AUTHOR'S IDENTITY

408.   Gardner, Helen L. "Walter Hilton and the Authorship of
        The Cloud of Unknowing." *RES*, 9 (1933), 129-47.

        A refutation of the hypothesis that Hilton authored the

Cloud. Gardner summarizes prior scholarship on the question, including that of Justin McCann and Maurice Noetinger, and carefully assesses manuscript evidence; seeming similarities of sources, style, and content; the chronology of the works; the psychology and personality of Hilton and the *Cloud* author. She concludes that Hilton could not be the author of the *Cloud*, which she places as an intermediate work between Rolle and Hilton. See her review of Hodgson's critical edition of *The Cloud of Unknowing and the Book of Privy Counseling*, *MA*, 16 (1947), 36-42, in which she alters her 1933 position, as outlined above, to one of uncertainty about the matter.

408a. Gatto, Louis C. "The Walter Hilton--*Cloud of Unknowing* Authorship Controversy Reconsidered." *Studies in Medieval Culture*, 5 (1975), 181-9.

Largely a recapitulation of past scholarship on the controversy. Gatto studies *Of Angels' Song*, *Mixed Life*, and the *Scale*, and concludes that Hilton's basic Christo-centricity is far removed from the theocentric *Cloud*, although he admits that the question remains unanswered.

409. Hodgson, Phyllis. "Walter Hilton and *The Cloud of Un-knowing*: A Problem of Authorship Reconsidered." *MLR*, 50 (1955), 395-406.

A reassessment of the Hilton/*Cloud* authorship problem and an argument for a separate authorship. Hodgson explains the seeming similarities as borrowings from a common medieval mystical background, and sees real differences in the handling of material, manifest not only in the divergent thought processes at work in the two writings, but also in the prose style.

410. Noetinger, Maurice. "The Authorship of *The Cloud of Unknowing*." *Blackfriars*, 4 (1924), 1457-64.

Noetinger explores and rejects the claim that the *Cloud* was written by Hilton or by a cloistered contemplative monk. He suggests the possibility of a Scottish author, based on a possible reference to the Scottish crown in the *Epistle of Discretion of Stirrings*. He also discounts any influence by the Continental mystics.

411. Peers, E. Allison. *Behind That Wall*. [England]: SCM Press, Ltd., 1947.

A collection of essays on the classics of the interior life, with a study on the *Cloud* and its author.

412. Riehle, Wolfgang. "The Problem of Walter Hilton's
      Possible Authorship of *The Cloud of Unknowing* and its
      Related Tracts." *NM*, 78 (1977), 31-45.

      Based on similarities of vocabulary, style, doctrinal
      variations, and provenance (NE Midland), Riehle theorizes
      that Hilton could have written the *Cloud*, but stipulates
      that further manuscript evidence is needed.

                    C. CRITICAL STUDIES OF THE WORKS

413. Bosse, Roberta Bux. "Mysticism and Huswifery in *Hali
      Meiðhad*." *FCEMN*, 2/4 (1976), 8-15.

      A delightful piece, showing "a sense of humanity" in
      the treatise, as well as serious spiritual reading,
      comparable, in parts, to that of the *Cloud*.

414. Brian, Dianne. "A Study of Imagery in *The Cloud of
      Unknowing*." Diss. Duke Univ. 1961. Kentucky Micro-
      cards Series A. Modern Language Series No. 93.

      A useful study of imagery for teachers of the *Cloud*,
      along with an analysis of the *Cloud*'s philosophical
      background.

415. Burrow, J.A. "Fantasy and Language in *The Cloud of
      Unknowing*." *EIC*, 27 (1977), 283-98.

      An exploration of the *Cloud* author's use of "bodily"
      language to depict the physical and spiritual worlds.
      Of worth is the discussion of the "homely," "physical,"
      "concrete" imagery which the *Cloud* author shares with
      nearly all Middle English mystical writers.

416. Cardiff, Ethelbert. "A Mystical Bypass of Christianity."
      CR, 23 (1943), 305-14.

      A refutation of Aldous Huxley's theses that Catholicism
      and mysticism are fundamentally incompatible, and that
      Indian and Christian mystics mean the same thing.
      Cardiff especially attacks Huxley's misreading and mis-
      application of the *Cloud*'s teaching.

417. Clark, J.P.H. "*The Cloud of Unknowing*, Walter Hilton,
      and St. John of the Cross: A Comparison." *DR*, 96
      (1978), 281-98.

After viewing the similarity of doctrine and expression in the three cited authors, and considering the possibility of influence from the Rhineland mystics and from the Carmelites, Clark concludes that the points of similarity can be ascribed to a "common tradition of contemplative spirituality."

417a. ————. "Sources and Theology in *The Cloud of Unknowing*." *DR*, 98 (1980), 83-109.

A careful assessment of sources for the *Cloud* corpus, leading to a hypothesis of mutual influence between the *Cloud* and Hilton's *Scale*. Specifically, Clark points to the likelihood that Book I of the *Scale* preceded the *Cloud*, while Book II of the *Scale* may have been influenced by the *Cloud*.

418. Conn, Joann Wolski. "Call and Response in *The Cloud of Unknowing*." *Contemplative Review*, 10 (1977), 27-30.

A useful and succinct analysis of the text of the *Cloud*, together with examples of its medieval cultural characteristics.

419. Egan, Harvey D. "Christian Apophatic and Kataphatic Mysticisms." *Theological Studies*, 39 (1978), 399-426.

This article maintains that genuine Christian mysticism must encompass apophatic (*via negativa*) and cataphatic (*via affirmativa*) elements. After giving a concise overview of modern Eastern and Western attitudes toward mysticism, Egan proceeds to substantiate his contention, based on an assessment of the *Cloud* and the Ignatian *Spiritual Exercises*, but also outlines the strengths and weaknesses of each tradition.

420. Elwin, V. *Christian Dhyāna or Prayer of Loving Regard: A Study of The Cloud of Unknowing*. New York: Macmillan, 1930.

A contribution to East-West dialogue on the mystics.

421. Grady, Sr. Laureen. "Afterword to *A Pistle of Discrecioun of Stirings*." *Contemplative Review*, 10 (1977), 1-6.

Shows how the wisdom and spiritual guidance of the author of the *Pistle* has a special relevance for those drawn to the contemplative life today.

422. Hort, Greta. *Sense and Thought: A Study in Mysticism.*
      London: George Allen & Unwin, Ltd., 1936.

      An excellent study centered around the *Cloud.*

423. Johnston, William. *The Mysticism of The Cloud of Un-
      knowing: A Modern Interpretation.* Foreword by Thomas
      Merton. St. Meinrad, Ind.: Abbey Press, 1975.

      A reprint of the 1965 edition, this study treats all
      seven works attributed to the *Cloud* author under the
      headings of Knowledge, Love, Purification, and Union,
      stressing the apophatic mystical tradition.

424. Jones, John D. "The Character of the Negative (Mystical)
      Theology for Pseudo-Dionysius Areopagite." In *Ethical
      Wisdom, East and/or West. Proceedings of the American
      Catholic Philosophical Assn.*, 51 (1977), 66-74.

      An excursus on the conception of negative, mystical
      theology developed by Ps.-Dionysius as it dominated
      medieval thought. It is not, according to Jones, com-
      petitive with affirmative theology, but is intertwined
      with it. A useful study in connection with the *Cloud.*

425. Knowles, David. "The Excellence of the *Cloud.*" *DR*, 52
      (1934), 71-92.

      Analyzes the unique excellence of the *Cloud* and the
      Epistle of Privy Counsel as treatises of mystical
      theology, especially because these works are being read
      and often misunderstood by those lacking the "acquired
      knowledge of traditional theology and the infused know-
      ledge of contemplation." Knowles particularly discusses
      the *Cloud*'s treatment of love, knowledge, and the life
      of grace.

426. McCann, Justin. "The Cloud of Unknowing." *Ampleforth
      Journal*, 29 (1924), 192-7.

      A percipient survey of theories and conjectures re-
      garding the author of the *Cloud*, concluding with McCann's
      preference for Walter Hilton.

427. McIntyre, David M. *"The Cloud of Unknowing." Expositor*,
      7th series, 22 (1907), 373-84.

      A general study of the work.

428. Martin, Denise. *"Le Nuage de l'inconnaissance." VS*,
      13 (1977), 660-82.

A discussion of the influences which inspired the work, especially the apophatic theology of Ps.-Dionysius, along with a parallel study of the *Cloud* and Zen.

429. Nieva, Constantino S. *This Transcending God*. London: The Mitre Press, 1971.

A broad introduction to the seven works commonly attributed to the *Cloud* author, with a major focus on the *Cloud*. Stresses questions of theology and mystical experience.

430. ———. "*The Cloud of Unknowing* and St. John of the Cross." *Mount Carmel*, 26 (1978), 79-89.

Investigates the possible likenesses and dissimilarities between the mystical theology of the *Cloud* author and St. John of the Cross, as expressed in his *Ascent to Mount Carmel*.

431. ———. "*The Cloud of Unknowing* and St. John of the Cross." *Mount Carmel*, 27 (1979), 182-91.

This article, in many ways a continuation of the foregoing study (430), compares the teaching of the *Cloud* and St. John of the Cross's *Dark Night of the Soul*, *Spiritual Canticles*, and *Living Flame of Love*, and concludes that John did not necessarily draw from the *Cloud*. Nieva also explores definitions of mystical theology, and the lessons on the *via mystica* taught by the *Cloud* author and St. John of the Cross.

432. O'Donoghue, Noel. "This Noble Noughting and This High Alling: Self-Relinquishment in *The Cloud of Unknowing* and the *Epistle of Privy Counsel*." *Journal of Studies in Mysticism*, 2 (1979), 1-15.

A discussion of the four liberations involved in the mystical process: from the world of the senses, from possession and possessions, from dogma, all of which are subsumed in the cloud of forgetting, and finally from the thought and feeling of one's own being, which is the "noble noughting and high alling," through the efficacy of divine grace, which is available in some measure to every man.

433. Smith, Graham. "The Prayer of Continual Turning Towards God." *DR*, 89 (1971), 153-7.

Outlines the *via negativa* method of prayer prescribed by the *Cloud* author, Augustine Baker, and others.

434. Walsh, James. *"The Cloud of Unknowing." Month,* 30
         (1963), 325-36.

         Recommending the *Cloud* to those who are actives in
         their outward form of living, Walsh clearly presents
         the teachings of the *Cloud* and associated tracts. This
         study is especially useful for its explanations of such
         terms as *synderesis* and *scintilla,* and is intended to
         encourage the practice of the *Cloud*'s way to God.

435. Zinn, Grover A., Jr. "Personification Allegory and
         Visions of Light in Richard of St. Victor's Teaching
         on Contemplation." *University of Toronto Quarterly,*
         46 (1977), 190-214.

         A penetrating study of Richard of St. Victor's
         Benjamin Minor and *Benjamin Major,* which serves as an
         excellent background for the *Cloud* author's canon.

IV. WALTER HILTON

Walter Hilton, an Augustinian Canon at Thurgarton (d. 1395/6) not only authored *The Scale of Perfection*, acknowledged as the most complete spiritual guide to the *via mystica* in the English mystical corpus, and several other works in the vernacular, but also a number of Latin works, the majority of which are unedited.

This section of the bibliography will consider:

A. Latin Writings
B. Editions of English Writings.
C. Doubtful Works.
D. Critical Studies.

A. LATIN WRITINGS
De Imagine Peccati; Epistola ad Quemdam Saeculo Renunciare Volentem; Epistola ad Solitarium de Lectione, Intentione, Oratione et Aliis; Epistola de Utilitate et Prerogativis Religionis; De Adoracione Imaginum

436. Kirchberger, Clare. "Scruples at Confession: A Modern English Translation of Part of the *Epistola ad Quemdam Saeculo Renunciare Volentem*." *LS*, 10 (1956), 451-6, 504-9.

Drawn from MS. B.L. Add. 33971.

437. Russell-Smith, Joy. "Walter Hilton and a Tract in Defense of the Veneration of Images." *Dominican Studies*, 7 (1954), 180-214.

An important study in which Russell-Smith carefully substantiates evidence for Hilton's authorship of the treatise *De Adoracione Imaginum*, based on similarities between the treatise and Hilton's established canon, as

well as other criteria. Also provides a survey of
Hilton's unpublished Latin minor works, and points to
his Carmelite and Carthusian connections.

438. ———. "A Letter to a Hermit." *Way*, 6 (1966), 230-41.

A modern English translation of the *Epistola ad Quemdam
Solitarium*, one of four Latin works in MS. B.L. Royal
6 E. III, with a brief preface.

B. ENGLISH WRITINGS
Of Angels' Song (H1, pp. 175-82);
On the Mixed Life (H1, pp. 264-92);
Eight Chapters on Perfection; *The
Goad of Love*; *The Scale of Perfec-
tion*, Books I and II.

439. Jones, Dorothy, ed. *Minor Works of Walter Hilton*.
London: Burns, Oates & Washbourne, Ltd., 1929.

This important anthology contains an introduction on
the manuscript tradition and printed versions, as well
as modernized texts of *On the Mixed Life*, *Eight Chapters
on Perfection*, *Qui Habitat*, *Bonum Est*, and *Benedictus*.
(Note: On the last three texts, see "Doubtful Works"
below.)

Of Angels' Song

440. Noetinger, Maurice, trans. *"Le Chant des Anges."* *VS*,
9 (1923-4), 72-9.

A French translation, with introduction.

441. Strakosch, Elisabeth, trans. *"Vom Engelgesang."*
Augustinana, 17 (1967), 443-7.

A German translation.

442. Takamiya, Toshiyuke, ed. *Of Angels' Song*. Studies in
English Literature. Tokyo, 1977, pp. 3-31.

A critical edition, based on MS. B.L. Add. 27952,
heretofore unnoted by Hilton scholars, with an introduction dealing with the manuscript tradition, previous
editions, and authorship; variants; glossary; and an
appendix of comparative parallel readings, corresponding

to lines 1-12 of this edition. See P.J.C. Field's review
in *FCEMN*, 5/2 (1979), 36-8.

On the Mixed Life

443. Strakosch, Elisabeth, trans. "Eine Epistel die *Von
    gemischten Leben*, handelt von Walter Hilton."
    Augustinana, 17 (1967), 299-326.

    A German translation, with introduction.

Eight Chapters on Perfection (translated from a Latin
    work of Louis de Fontibus)

444. Kuriyagawa, Fumio, ed. *The Paris Manuscript of Walter
    Hilton's Eight Chapters on Perfection.* Tokyo: Keio
    University, 1958.

    A critical edition of the Middle English text, based
    on MS. B.N. anglais 41, with variants from manuscripts
    at Oxford and Cambridge, and an introduction on the
    manuscript tradition and language of the text.

445. ———. *Walter Hilton's Eight Chapters on Perfection.*
    Tokyo: The Keio Institute of Cultural and Linguistic
    Studies, 1967.

    A completely revised and enlarged form of the author's
    1958 edition, based on all known manuscripts of the
    work, with textual notes, glossary, bibliography, and
    illustrative plates.

446. ———. "The Inner Temple Manuscript of Walter Hilton's
    Eight Chapters on Perfection." *Studies in English
    Literature* (Tokyo). English Number 1971, pp. 7-34.

The Goad of Love (translation of James of Milan's
    Stimulus Amoris)

447. James of Milan. *Stimulus Amoris Fr. Jacobi Mediolanen-
    sis: Canticum Pauperis Fr. Johannis Peckham.* Ed. PP.
    Collegii S. Bonaventurae. Bibliotheca Franciscana
    Ascetica Medii Aevi, Tomus 4. Quaracchi, 1905.

    Contains the Latin text of the *Stimulus Amoris* and the
    attribution to James of Milan.

448. Kane, Harold J. "A Critical Edition of the *Prickynge*

of Love." Diss. Univ. of Pennsylvania 1968.

An edition based on MS. B.L. Harl. 2254. Kane holds
that Hilton's authorship is possible, but not proven.

449. Kirchberger, Clare, ed. *The Goad of Love*. New York:
Harper and Brothers, 1951; London: Faber and Faber,
1952.

A modernized text of Walter Hilton's Middle English
translation of the *Stimulus Amoris* of James of Milan,
formerly attributed to St. Bonaventure. With an excellent introduction on the manuscript tradition, Hilton's
life, the cultural and religious milieux of late 14th-
century England, and a careful assessment of Hilton's
adaptation of the Latin work.

The Scale of Perfection--Early Editions

450. *Scala Perfectionis*. London: Wynkyn de Worde, 1494;
1525 (STC 14044); 1533 (STC 14045).

451. *Scala Perfectionis*. London: Julian Notary, 1507 (STC
14043).

452. *To a devoute man in temporall estate, howe he should
rule hym*. London: Rycharde Pynson, 1506; 1516.

453. *The Scale (or Ladder) of Perfection, Written by Walter
Hilton*. Printed first in the yeare 1494. By the
changing of some antiquated words, rendered more in-
telligible. London: T.R., 1659.

This is the Augustine Baker/Serenus Cressy edition.

The Scale of Perfection--Modern Editions

454. *The Scale of Perfection*, with an introductory essay on
"The Spiritual Life of Medieval England," by John
D.B. Dalgairns. A reprinting of the 1659 edition.
London: J. Philp, 1870; rpt. London: Art and Book Co.,
1901.

Dalgairn's essay stresses the interrelationship of
the spiritual and social life of England in the Middle
Ages and, although somewhat dated, remains a perceptive
study of the period.

454a. Birts, Rosemary. "An Edition of Chaps. 38 to 52 of
Hilton's *Scale of Perfection*, Book I." M. Litt.
Thesis Oxford Univ. 1951.

455. del Mastro, M.L., ed. *The Stairway of Perfection*.
Garden City, N.Y.: Doubleday & Company, Inc., 1979.

A Modern English version of the *Scale*, with an extensive introduction which includes a helpful guide to the
reading of the work, based on del Mastro's conception
of Hilton's order of ascent as a spiral staircase.

456. Hussey, Stanley S. "An Edition from the Manuscripts
of Book II of Walter Hilton's *Scale of Perfection*."
Diss. Univ. of London, Bedford College 1962.

457. Noetinger, Maurice, and E. Bouvet, eds. *L'Echelle de la
Perfection*. Tours: A. Mame et Fils, 1923.

A French translation, with an outstanding introduction
by Noetinger concerning Hilton, his milieu, his position
among the 14th-century English mystics, informing influences on his writings, and an analysis of the *Scale*.

458. Oblate of Solesmes, ed. *The Scale of Perfection*. Introduction from the French of M. Noetinger. London:
Burns, Oates & Washbourne, Ltd., 1927.

A partially modernized version, with Noetinger's introduction.

459. Sherley-Price, Leo, ed. *The Ladder of Perfection*.
Harmondsworth, Middlesex: Penguin Books, 1957.

A modernized translation, drawn from the Evelyn
Underhill edition (see 463 below), with introduction
and notes.

460. ————. *The Scale of Perfection by Walter Hilton*.
Abridged and introduced by Dom Illtyd Trethowan.
St. Meinrad, Ind.: Abbey Press, 1975.

This is a reissue of Price's largely accurate 1957
translation, with Trethowan's abridgement and commentary.
Contains 18 chapters of the 93 which compose Book I,
and 35 of the 43 chapters of Book II. Stresses the
importance of Hilton's teaching for today's non-
specialized reader, with the effect of minimizing
Hilton's relationship to his own age.

461. Sitwell, Gerard, ed. *The Scale of Perfection*. London:
     Burns, Oates; Westminster, Md.: The Newman Press,
     1953.

     A modern English version, drawn from Evelyn Under-
     hill's 1923 edition, and checked against the Orchard
     Series text of Wynkyn de Worde's 1494 edition, with
     helpful explanatory notes and commentary on Hilton's
     theology, terminology, and teaching. The introduction
     contains an informative section (No. 3) on the spiri-
     tuality of the *Scale*, and a guide to the reading of
     the work.

462. Strakosch, Elisabeth, ed. *Glaube und Erfahrung*. Intro-
     duction by Hans Urs von Balthasar. Einsiedeln:
     Johannesverlag, 1966.

463. Underhill, Evelyn, ed. *The Scale of Perfection*. Lon-
     don: John M. Watkins, 1923; rpt. 1948.

     The introduction discusses Hilton's milieu, the major
     informing influences on his writings (among them Augus-
     tine, Richard of St. Victor, and the *Cloud* author), the
     question of Hilton's authorship of the *Cloud*, and a
     helpful analysis of the *Scale*'s teachings. The modernized
     text, based primarily on MS. B.L. Harl. 6579, is directed
     toward the general reader and persons interested in
     Christian mysticism.

464. Wykes, Barbara E. "Edition of Book I of *The Scale of
     Perfection* by Walter Hilton." Diss. Univ. of Michigan
     1958.

     A semi-diplomatic reproduction of MS. B.L. Harl.
     6579, with an introduction on the history of Book I,
     Hilton's mysticism and literary style, and an analysis
     of the Middle English dialect, with Wykes holding that
     Hilton wrote in the Northeast Midland or Northern dia-
     lect, while the scribe used the Southeast Midland dia-
     lect.

C. DOUBTFUL WORKS
Commentaries on Psalm 90 (*Qui
Habitat*) and Psalm 91 (*Bonum Est*),
and the *Benedictus*.

Qui Habitat and Bonum Est

465. Wallner, Björn, ed. *An Exposition of Qui Habitat and
Bonum Est in English.* Lund Studies in English 23.
Lund: C.W.K. Gleerup, 1954.

A critical edition of these two texts, based primarily
on the Vernon manuscript, with introduction, notes, and
glossary. Anna Paues had ascribed these texts to Rolle
or his school. Dorothy Jones in *Minor Works of Walter
Hilton* (see 439) attributed authorship to Hilton, while
Evelyn Underhill, in her review of Jones's work in
Spectator, June 8, 1929, doubts that Hilton wrote the
Bonum Est. Wallner compares the two texts with each
other, as well as other Hilton works, and concludes
that, while the external evidence is slight, internal
evidence does point to his authorship.

466. Ekwall, Eilert. "The Manuscript Collections of the late
Professor Anna Paues." *Studia Neophilologica*, 21
(1948-49), 23-41.

An inventory of Dr. Paues's manuscript research collection, deposited at Lund University, which includes much
material on Middle English biblical versions and related
matters, as well as meditations on Psalms 90 and 91,
which Paues had hoped to prove were by the hand of Rolle.

Benedictus

467. Wallner, Björn, ed. *A Commentary on the Benedictus.*
Lund, 1957.

A critical edition, based on MS. Lambeth 472, with
variant readings from MS. Newcastle. Wallner finds
external and internal evidence of Hilton's authorship
to be inconclusive.

468. Colledge, E. "The English Prose *Benedictus*: A Second
Manuscript." *MA*, 8 (1939), 45-9.

Reports on a new Middle English version of the *Benedictus* in a Newcastle Public Library manuscript, which
affords several readings preferable to MS. Lambeth 472,

but does not solve the problem of authorship by Rolle or
Hilton.

D. CRITICAL STUDIES

469. Beale, Walter H. "Walter Hilton and the Concept of the
      'Medled Lyf.'" *ABR*, 26 (1975), 381-94.

      Beale's major contention is that the topic of the
      active and contemplative life in the Middle Ages was
      not essentially a set of names for the church hierarchy,
      or for steps in spiritual perfection, or for alternative
      lifestyles. Rather, "it was primarily a set of open-
      ended antitheses, accompanied by a vast biblical sym-
      bolism, including in its semantic well ... the whole
      structure of the Christian community, the human personali-
      ty, history, and the order of the world." The terms were
      therefore an incentive for meditation on "the duality
      that underlies existence itself."

470. Bliss, A.J. "Two Hilton Manuscripts in Columbia Univer-
      sity Library." *MA*, 38 (1969), 157-63.

      Concludes that Plimpton's MSS. 257 (*The Scale of Per-
      fection*) and 271 (*Mixed Life*) once formed part of a
      single codex.

471. Clark, J.P.H. "The 'Lightsome Darkness'--Aspects of
      Walter Hilton's Theological Background." *DR*, 95 (1977),
      95-109.

      This article supplements Phyllis Hodgson's study of
      stylistic differences between the *Scale* and other works
      ascribed to Hilton, and *The Cloud of Unknowing* and its
      related works (see 393-4). Clark focusses on the dif-
      ferent theologies and the sources therefor underlying
      the *Cloud* and *Scale*, and concludes that the work of
      English language scholars who have rejected Hilton's
      authorship of the *Cloud* is borne out on theological
      grounds. Also holds that the authorship of *Bonum Est*
      and *Qui Habitat* remains uncertain.

472. ————. "Walter Hilton and 'Liberty of Spirit.'" *DR*,
      96 (1978), 61-78.

      Incisively assesses Walter Hilton's English and Latin
      writings, showing that not only were they intended as

correctives to Rolle's sense-oriented enthusiasm, but,
even more, were concerned with combatting Wycliffite
anti-sacramental tenets and the Continental "Free Spirit"
heresy promulgated by the Beghards and typified by Margaret Porete's *Mirror of Simple Souls*.

473. ————. "Intention in Walter Hilton." *DR*, 97 (1979),
      69-80.

Hilton's teaching gives witness to a persistent element
in medieval theology: the stress on the dynamic power of
intention and the primacy of will and love. The same
emphasis emerges in Julian of Norwich and the *Cloud*.
Clark also shows links between some fine points of Hilton's teaching and concepts in Abelard, Bonaventure,
and Duns Scotus.

474. ————. "Image and Likeness in Walter Hilton." *DR*, 97
      (1979), 204-20.

This study explores the conservative Augustinian influences which pervade *The Scale of Perfection*. Clark
traces the sources for Hilton's understanding of the
soul as created "Imago Dei," but, owing to the Fall,
filled with "Imago Peccati." Through contemplation, we
break through the "Imago Peccati," and the soul is re-
stored to its original likeness of God, which, for
Hilton, is expressed in the twin virtues of humility
and charity.

475. ————. "Action and Contemplation in Walter Hilton."
      DR, 97 (1979), 258-74.

This study explores Book II of the *Scale* to show Hilton's changing view of contemplation as a spiritual
course open to all Christians, and his reliance for this
view on such sources as Gregory, Cassian, Augustine,
William of St. Thierry, Hugh of St. Victor, and Thomas
Aquinas.

476. Coleman, Thomas W. "Walter Hilton's *Scale of Perfec-
      tion*." *LQHR*, 160 (1935), 241-5.

A study of Hilton, the man and the cleric, as well as
sources of and informing influences on his work, along
with an analysis of the *Scale*.

477. Colledge, E. "Recent Work on Walter Hilton." *Black-
      friars*, 37 (1956), 265-70.

This article surveys and commends past scholarship on

Hilton by Dorothy Jones, Clare Kirchberger, Joy Russell-Smith, Björn Wallner, Gerard Sitwell, and Margaret Deanesly, but stresses the need for continuing adequate studies of Hilton's works, and namely the unedited, unpublished Latin works, and a critical edition of the *Scale*. Colledge concludes that Hilton's works manifest change and development in the author's thought, doctrine, and style, and that continuing investigation of the *Scale* and minor works will show that Hilton was not the author of *The Cloud of Unknowing*.

478. De Montmorency, J.E.G. "Master Walter Hilton and the Authorship of the *Imitation*." In *Thomas a Kempis, His Age and His Book*. London: Methuen and Co., 1906, pp. 139-69.

Contains a full discussion of the tradition that Hilton was the author of the first three books of the *Imitation of Christ*, which circulated in England under the title *De Ecclesiastica Musica*.

479. de Moustier, Benôit. "Doctor Discretus: Walter Hilton." *C&C*, 11 (1959), 292-300.

Upholds Hilton as "the doctor of moderation" in matters of the *via mystica*, and stresses the necessity of negative and positive asceticism.

480. Gardner, Helen L. "The Text of *The Scale of Perfection*." *MA*, 5 (1936), 11-30.

Examines the process of revising and adaption which marked the *Scale* from its first appearance, and continued throughout the centuries. Book I was revised, possibly by Hilton, through Christocentric additions, while Book II remained unchanged. Gardner holds that, while the passage on the Holy Name in Book I is genuine, the additions were not made by Hilton, but were glosses added either at Syon Abbey or Sheen Charterhouse. Gardner also suggests that Book I and Book II were meant to stand as separate works.

481. ————. "Walter Hilton and the Mystical Tradition of England." *Essays and Studies by Members of the English Association*, 22 (1936), 103-27.

An extended discussion of Walter Hilton's works, especially the *Scale*, and his indebtedness to the Fathers, the *Vitae Patrum*, the Victorines, Bernard, Anselm, the

Ancrene Riwle, Rolle, and the *Cloud* author. Gardner also traces Hilton's ongoing popularity with the post-Reformation recusants.

482. Hughes, Albert C. *Walter Hilton's Directions to Contemplatives*. Rome: Typis Pontificae Universitatis Gregoriana, 1962.

An excellent assessment of Hilton's theology, with an extensive bibliography.

483. Hussey, Stanley S. "The Text of *The Scale of Perfection*, Book II." *NM*, 65 (1964), 75-92.

A progress report on the critical edition of Book II, which Professor Hussey is undertaking, including a list of printed editions and modernizations, extant manuscripts, and the manuscript problems which have led Hussey to use MS. B.L. Harl. 6579 as the copy text for Book II.

484. ———. "Latin and English in *The Scale of Perfection*." *MS*, 35 (1973), 456-76.

An analysis of the Latin texts of Book II of the *Scale*, as well as a comparative study of the Latin and English texts, concluding with the need to consider the Latin text authority in any critical edition of the work.

485. Kennedy, David G. "The Incarnational Element in the Spirituality of Walter Hilton." Diss. McGill Univ. 1979.

Kennedy studies changes in Hilton's spirituality as a result of his deepening awareness of the doctrine of the Incarnation, and argues that Hilton's works can be arranged chronologically as they evince this Christological awareness.

486. Mabry, Paul E. "The Mystical Life in Walter Hilton." Diss. Temple Univ. 1971.

In explaining the key passages of the *Scale*, Mabry indicates how they differ significantly from the traditional interpretations, and suggests possible causes for Hilton's purpose and employment of language, terms, and literary devices. According to Mabry, Hilton attempts to go beyond devotional piety and transcendental experience, and seeks religious reality in this life, with conformed love as the ground of all being and

thereby the reality of life. Hence, the religious life
is the life of love.

487. McSorley, Joseph. *"The Scale of Perfection."* *NCW*, 74
      (1901-2), 33-46.

      An apologia for Hilton as a true representative of
      Roman Catholic orthodoxy-cum-sanctity during the 14th
      century, and an insistence on the universal appeal of
      the *Scale*.

488. Milosh, Joseph E. *The Scale of Perfection and the
      English Mystical Tradition.* Madison, Milwaukee,
      London: Univ. of Wisconsin Press, 1966.

      An analysis of the *Scale* to inculcate an appreciation
      of Hilton's teachings and methods, and of his place as
      the "principal contemplative of the 14th-century English
      school." Special attention is given to Hilton's instruc-
      tions on the active and contemplative life, and to Hil-
      ton's treatment of the seven deadly sins as obstacles
      to contemplation. Milosh finds the *Scale* a unified, ef-
      fective, practical guide to contemplation. See his
      "An Analysis of Walter Hilton's Teachings in *The Scale
      of Perfection*." Diss. Univ. of Illinois 1963.

489. Noetinger, Maurice. "Le contemplation d'après Hilton."
      VS, 4 (1920-1), 453-9.

      Seeks to establish Hilton as the continuator of Hugh
      and Richard of St. Victor by an analysis of the *Scale*.

490. ————. "The Modern Editions of Walter Hilton's *Scala
      Perfectionis*." *DR*, 41 (1923), 149-57.

      The author compares modern editions, all of which are
      based on the 1659 edition of Augustine Baker and Serenus
      Cressy, with Wynkyn de Worde's 1494 edition, and finds
      many textual alterations and misinterpretations in the
      1659 edition, which point to the need for a critical
      edition of the *Scale*.

491. Owen, H.P. "Christian Mysticism: A Study in Walter
      Hilton's *The Ladder of Perfection*." *Religious
      Studies*, 7 (1971), 31-42.

      Assessing the interpenetration of Christian dogma and
      mystical experience in the *Scale*, Owen refutes the thesis,
      represented in Ninian Smart's article "Interpenetration
      and Religious Experience," *Religious Studies*, 1 (1965),

that the experience of all mystics are phenomenological-
ly identical, whether panenhenic, monistic, or theistic.

492. Pankhurst, C.K. "The Active Life, the Contemplative
Life, and the Mixed Life--A Study of the Three Lives
with Special Reference to Walter Hilton." Diss. Univ.
of York 1976.

An exploration of the concept of the mixed life as
expounded by Augustine, Gregory the Great, and Bernard
of Clairvaux, as well as other writers of the 12th,
13th, and 14th centuries, and as adapted by Hilton in
his *Scale* and *Epistle on the Mixed Life*.

493. Pepler, Conrad. "*The Scale*." *LS*, 3 and 4 (1949), 504-
11.

This is the last in a series of articles concerning
the mystics from the standpoint of the development of
the soul under grace, as recorded by William Langland,
the *Ancrene Riwle*, Rolle, the *Cloud* author, Julian of
Norwich, and Hilton. Hilton alone records the whole
way of progress to union, according to Pepler, who gives
a clear analysis of the way as presented in the *Scale*.

494. Russell-Smith, Joy. "Walter Hilton." *Month*, 207, N.S.
21 (1959), 133-48.

A discussion of Hilton's attitude toward the active,
contemplative, and mixed life, based on his English
and Latin writings and his translation of the *Stimulus
Amoris*. The study outlines differences between Books I
and II of the *Scale*, seen in the implied audience of
each book, the author's growth in self-assurance, the
greater theological content of Book II, and its relevance for the spiritual guidance of all men. Russell-
Smith concludes with Hilton's additions to his translation of the *Stimulus*, which hold that the illuminative
life appears under two normal forms, contemplative and
active.

495. Sitwell, Gerard. "Contemplation in *The Scale of Perfection*." *DR*, 67 (1949), 276-90; 68 (1950), 21-34;
and 69 (1950), 271-89.

This tripartite study is a detailed examination of the
Scale, showing that in its broad outlines, Hilton's
description of contemplation conforms exactly to that
of later writers such as St. Teresa of Avila and St.
John of the Cross. Sitwell also compares the *Scale* with
the *Cloud*.

496.   ――――. "English Spiritual Writers VII. Walter Hilton."
       CR, 44 (1959), 321-32.

       A study of Hilton's spirituality as expressed in the
       Scale.

497.   Takamiya, Toshiyuki. "A Hilton Manuscript Once in the
       Possession of Luttrell Wynne." *Reports of the Keio
       Institute of Cultural and Linguistic Studies*, 7 (1975),
       171-91.

       A report on the Wynn codex, together with a list of
       60 manuscripts of English and Latin versions of the
       Scale.

V. JULIAN OF NORWICH

Julian of Norwich (1343-1415?) wrote two
versions of her *Revelations of Divine
Love* or *Showings*: the Short Version, composed after her series of sixteen mystical
visions which occurred in 1373; and the
Long Version, written after twenty years
of meditation and contemplation.

This section of the bibliography will
consider:
A. Editions.
B. Critical Studies.

A. EDITIONS

498. *Revelations to One Who Could Not Read a Letter.* A
photographic facsimile of MS. B.L. Sloane 2499,
Modern Language Association of America Collection
No. 312 (1935), deposited in the Library of Congress.

499. *Liber Revelacionum Julyane, Anacorite Norwyche.* A
photographic facsimile of MS. B.N. Fonds anglais 40,
Modern Language Association of America Collection No.
315 (1935), deposited in the Library of Congress.

500. *Revelations of the Unutterable Love of God in Jesus
Christ, Vouchsafed to a Dear Lover of His and in Her
to All His Dear Friends and Lovers.* A photographic
facsimile of MS. B.L. Sloane 3705, Modern Language
Association of America Collection No. 320 (1935),
deposited in the Library of Congress.

501. *Revelations of Divine Love.* London: Methuen & Co., 1934.

502. Allen, Sr. M. Edwards. "Dame Julian of Norwich's
Revelations of Divine Love (1373). An Edition with
Notes." Unpublished Master's Thesis, De Paul Univ.
1948.

503.   Baudry, Etienne, ed. *Une Révélation de l'amour de Dieu:*
        version brève des Deize révélations de l'amour de
        Dieu. Textes Monastique. Begrolles en Mauges (M. and
        L.), France: Abbaye de Bellefontaine, 1977.

        A French translation of Sr. Anna Marie Reynolds's
        Modern English version, *A Shewing of God's Love*, in-
        cluding her introduction. Baudry's own introduction
        discusses four traits of Julian's personality which
        inform her style and content: optimism, objectivity and
        realism, comprehension of faith, and sense of Christian
        community. Baudry feels Julian has a special relevance
        for women who are today seeking their role in the Church.
        Like Reynolds, Baudry has also appended a translation of
        the three chapters from the Long Version, dealing with
        the Motherhood of God.

504.   Beer, Frances, ed. *Revelations of Divine Love.* Heidel-
        berg: Carl Winter Universitätsverlag, 1978.

        A critical edition of the Short Version of Julian's
        Revelations, contained in MS. B.L. Add. 37790, with an
        excellent introduction on Julian, the manuscript tradi-
        tion, relationship of the Long and Short Versions, and
        an analysis of the work's subject matter.

505.   Bottoni, Pietro. *Rivelazioni dell'amore divino.* Rome:
        Editrice Studium, 1957.

        An Italian translation of the Long Version, based on
        Hudleston's Modern English text.

506.   Colledge, Edmund, and James Walsh, eds. *Showings.* New
        York: Paulist Press, 1978.

        A modern translation of the Short and Long Versions of
        Julian's *Revelations*, with a scholarly introduction dis-
        cussing textual, doctrinal, and thematic concerns.

507.   ————. *A Book of Shewings to the Anchoress Julian of*
        Norwich. 2 vols. Toronto: Pontifical Institute of
        Mediaeval Studies, 1978.

        The critical edition of the two versions of the *Revela-*
        tions, employing all known manuscripts. Vol. 1 contains
        a comprehensive study of the manuscript tradition, of
        Julian's milieu, of major informing influences on her
        theology and spirituality, an analysis of the work, and
        a text of the Short Version, drawn from the only extant
        manuscript, MS. B.L. Add. 37790. Vol. 2 contains the

Long Version, based on MS. B.N. Fonds anglais 40, collated with all other known manuscripts, including the Upholland Seminary Library text, and the 1670 Cressy
printed edition. Both versions are fully and informa-
tively annotated. See J.P.H. Clark's review in *DR*, 97
(1980), 69-72. Fr. Clark's insightful appraisal of this
important critical edition gently questions some of the
editors' specific source attributions, finding that
Julian could well have relied on Scriptures and long-
established Church teaching and traditions. He concludes: "Students of Julian will be warmly grateful for
this edition. The fact that in this review it has been
possible to put forward alternative suggestions at a
number of points only underlines the richness and deli-
cacy of Julian's theology." Also see Morton Bloomfield's
review in *Speculum*, 55 (1980), 548-9.

508. Collins, Henry, ed. *Revelations of Divine Love*. London:
     T. Richardson and Sons, 1877.

     From MS. B.L. Sloane 2499.

509. Congreve, George, ed. *The Showing of a Vision, being
     Extracts from Revelations of Divine Love Shewed to a
     Devout Anchoress by name Julian of Norwich*. London,
     1915.

     Excerpts from the *Revelations*.

510. Cressy, R.F.S., ed. *XVI Revelations of Divine Love,
     Shewed to a Devout Servant of Our Lord, Called Mother
     Juliana, an Anchorete of Norwich: Who Lived in the
     Dayes of King Edward the Third*. London, 1670 (Wing
     C6904); 2nd ed. London: S. Clarke, 1843.

     Using the Cressy text, G.H. Parker produced the second
     edition, under the title *Sixteen Revelations of Divine
     Love, made to a Devout Servant of Our Lord Called Mother
     Juliana of Norwich*. Leicester, 1843.

511. del Mastro, M.L., ed. *Revelations of Divine Love,
     Juliana of Norwich*. Garden City, N.Y.: Image Books,
     1977.

     Using the available manuscripts, del Mastro has pro-
     duced a Modern English edition of the Long Version for
     the non-specialist audience. Her introduction surveys
     the trends of the 14th-century and other English mystics,
     and offers guidelines for reading the *Revelations*.

512. De Luca, Maria, ed. *Rivelazioni dell'amore divino*.
      Torino: Società editrice internazionale, 1932.
      An Italian translation of the Long Version.

513. Glasscoe, Marion, ed. *A Revelation of Love*. Exeter
      Medieval Texts. Exeter: Univ. of Exeter Press, 1976.
      A student edition of the Long Version of the *Revela-
      tions* contained in MS. B.L. Sloane 2499, chosen as the
      base text because its language is much closer to 14th-
      century English. Contains an introduction, brief bibliog-
      raphy, and glossary. Recommended for students and for
      all those who wish to experience Julian's message in its
      own idiom. See Sr. Anna Maria Reynold's review in
      FCEMN, 3/2 (1977), 16-7.

514. Harford, Dundas, ed. *The Shewings of Lady Julian,
      Recluse at Norwich, 1373*. (Previously entitled *Com-
      fortable Words for Christ's Lovers*.) London: H.R.
      Allenson, 1911 and 1912; 3rd ed. London: H.R. Allenson;
      and Chicago: W.P. Blessing Co., 1925.

      A transcription of the Short Version, which Harford
      holds to be the original version.

515. Hecker, I.T., ed. *Sixteen Revelations of Divine Love,
      Made to a Devout Servant of Our Lord, Called Mother
      Juliana*. Boston: Ticknor and Fields, 1864.

      A modernized version of Serenus Cressy's edition.

516. Hudleston, Roger, ed. *Revelations of Divine Love Shewed
      to a Devout Ankress, by Dame Julian of Norwich*. Lon-
      don, 1927, 1935; 2nd ed. Westminster, Md.: Newman
      Press, 1952.

      A modernized edition of the Long Version, based on MS.
      B.L. Sloane 2499, with an informative introduction and
      guide to the reading of the *Revelations*, along with
      notes and a glossary.

517. Karrer, Otto, ed. *Offenbarungen der göttlichen Liebe*.
      Trans. George Gerlach. Paderborn: F. Schöningh, 1927.

518. Maisonneuve, Roland, ed. *Le Petit Livre des révélations,
      selon le manuscrit court du British Museum*. Haute-
      ville, Switzerland, and Paris: Editions du Parvis,
      1976.

      A sensitive, Modern French translation of the Short

Version of the *Revelations*. The introduction discusses
the historical Julian, as well as the themes, style, and
teachings of the work.

519. Meunier, Gabriel, ed. *Révélations de l'amour divin à*
Julienne de Norwich, recluse du XIV siècle. Paris:
1910; 2nd ed. A. Mame, 1925.

520. Reynolds, Frances (Sr. Anna Maria), ed. "An Edition of
MS. Sloane 2499 of Sixteen *Revelations of Divine Love*
by Julian of Norwich." Master's Thesis, Univ. of
Leeds 1947.

521. ———. "A Critical Edition of the *Revelations* of
Julian of Norwich (1342-c. 1416), Prepared from All
Known MSS." Diss. Univ. of Leeds 1956.

This edition contains an introduction, critical notes,
and a select glossary.

522. ———. *A Showing of God's Love; the Shorter Version*
of Sixteen Revelations of Divine Love. London and
New York: Longmans Green, 1958; Ann Arbor, Mich.:
Univ. Microfilms, 1973; London: Sheed and Ward, 1974.

From the Short Version in MS. B.L. 37790. Contains,
in addition, the chapters from the Long Version on the
Motherhood of God. A precise, yet readable modernization
of the original texts.

523. Sherley-Price, Leo, ed. *Lent With Mother Julian: An*
Anthology. London, 1962.

Extracts from the *Revelations*.

524. Strakosch, Elisabeth, trans. *Offenbarungen von göttlicher*
Liebe. Einsiedeln: Johannes Verlag, 1960.

A German translation of the *Revelations*.

525. Tyrrell, George, ed. *XVI Revelations of Divine Love*
Shewed to Mother Juliana of Norwich 1373. London:
Kegan Paul, Trench, Trübner & Co., 1902.

A Modernization of Cressy's 1670 edition, with a
preface by Tyrrell.

526. Walsh, James, ed. *The Revelations of Divine Love of*
Julian of Norwich. London and New York, 1961;
Wheathampstead, Herts.: Anthony Clark Books, 1973.

527. ————. *The Revelations of Divine Love of Julian of
      Norwich*. St. Meinrad, Ind.: Abbey Press, 1974, 1975.

      A modern edition of the Long Version, collated from
      MSS. B.L. Sloane 2499 and 3705 and B.N. Fonds anglais
      40, using the Paris manuscript as the base text. This
      reprint contains a new, extensive introduction, with an
      in-depth analysis of Julian's theology and teaching, and
      additional information about her forerunners.

528. Warrack, Grace, ed. *Revelations of Divine Love. Re-
      corded by Julian Anchoress at Norwich Anno Domini
      1373*. London: Methuen & Co., 1901; 13th ed., 1949;
      rpt. London: Methuen & Co., 1958.

      Valuable introductory notes on manuscripts and editors,
      and on the two Julians (Julian, anchoress at St. Julian's,
      and Juliana Lampit, anchoress at Carrow), showing that
      Julian is not Juliana Lampit. Further comments on
      Julian's life, on the inherently Christian content of
      her work, the main influences, and the themes of the
      Revelations of Divine Love.

529. Wolters, Clifton, ed. *Revelations of Divine Love*.
      Harmondsworth, Middlesex, and Baltimore: Penguin Books,
      1966, 1973.

      One of the best modernizations of the Long Version,
      based on MS. B.L. Sloane 2499, with an excellent intro-
      duction.

                         B. CRITICAL STUDIES

530. "Through Convent Windows: Heart of Grace." *Dublin Re-
      view*, 165 (1919), 290-307.

      An overview of medieval women mystics, with a dis-
      cussion of Julian, her *Revelations*, and her milieu.

531. Albert, Sr. Mary. "God is Our Mother." *LS*, 2 (1945),
      49-53.

      A brief, solid study of the metaphor of the Motherhood
      of God as found in Julian, and supported by related
      texts from Deuteronomy, Isaias, and the Gospels.

532. ————. "Spiritual Childhood and Mother Julian." *LS*,

2 (1945), 81-83.

Introduction to Julian's theme of spiritual childhood.

533. ———. "The Motherhood of God." *LS*, 7 (1952), 85-96.

Important explanatory essay on the tradition of the
metaphor of motherhood in mysticism, arguing for a
separate study of Julian's use of the metaphor.

534. Allchin, A.M. "Mother Julian of Norwich and Walsingham."
Walsingham Review, No. 44 (1972), pp. 7-12.

535. ———. "Julian of Norwich--Today." *FCEMN*, 6/1 (1980),
11-28.

An address at the Julian Sixth Centenary at Norwich
in 1973, stressing the importance of the contemplative
tradition and especially of Julian's message of love
for today's world.

536. ———, and Sisters of the Love of God. *Julian of Norwich: Four Studies to Commemorate the Sixth Centenary
of the Revelations of Divine Love*. Fairacres, Oxford:
S.L.G. Press, 1973; rpt. 1975.

An excellent general companion to the reading of
Julian's *Revelations*, with an introduction by A.M.
Allchin.

537. Baker, Albert E. "The Lady Juliana of Norwich." In
Prophets for a Day of Judgment. London: Eyre and
Spottiswoode, 1944; rpt. 1968, pp. 39-55.

A discussion of Julian's England and an analysis of
her *Revelations*.

538. Balfour, Charlotte. "The Anchoress." *NCW*, 109 (1919),
203-11.

A discussion of the life of the medieval anchoress as
revealed by the *Ancrene Riwle* and by Julian's *Revelations*,
expressing the spiritual heights which could be achieved
in the anchoritic state.

539. A Benedictine of Stanbrook. "Dame Julian of Norwich."
CR, 44 (1959), 705-20.

A discussion of "unlettered" Julian's learning, her
religious status, her essential orthodoxy, and the Short

and Long Versions of her *Revelations*, along with an
analysis of Margery Kempe's account of her meeting with
Julian.

540. Børresen, Kari Elizabeth. "Christ nôtre mère, la
      Théologie de Julienne de Norwich." *Mitteilungen und
      Forschungsbeitrage der Cusanus-Gesellschaft*, 13 (1978),
      320-9.

      An excellent study, showing the Scriptural and tradi-
      tional sources and theological implications of Julian's
      use of "mother" as a metaphor for Christ.

541. Bradley, Ritamary. "The Motherhood Theme in Julian of
      Norwich." *FCEMN*, 2/4 (1976), 25-30.

      A preliminary sketch of an article developed more
      fully in 542 below.

542. ─────. "Patristic Background of the Motherhood Simili-
      tude in Julian of Norwich." *Christian Scholar's Re-
      view*, 8 (1978), 101-13.

      The similitude of mother, applied to Christ and to
      the Trinity, is central to an understanding of Julian's
      treatise. Julian is using a well-known metaphor with
      centrally orthodox meanings in writing of her mystical
      experiences. The metaphor has an unbroken history in
      the patristic tradition. Although Cabussut (see 547)
      and others have noted some scattered patristic ante-
      cedents for the metaphor, this study supplies a continuity
      of uses, widespread in Augustine, anticipated as early
      as Philo, and echoed, with developments, to the time of
      Julian. The motherhood similitude signifies what
      Julian's type of Christian mysticism is essentially
      about.

543. Brégy, Katherine. "The Lady Anchoress." *NCW*, 135 (1932),
      9-15.

      A general discussion of the medieval anchoress in
      literature, leading up to a sensitive exploration of
      Julian's life and her *Revelations*.

544. Brinkworth, Guy. *"Thou Art Enough!" Julian of Norwich.*
      Birchington, Kent: Mullan Press, 1973.

      An excellent short introduction to the teaching of
      Julian, with aptly chosen quotations from her *Revela-
      tions*.

545. Busshart, Helen. "Julian of Norwich--God's Love and
     the Experience of Dying." *Contemplative Review*, 12
     (1979), 6-13; 13 (1980), 24-8.

     This two-part essay compares the near-death studies
     of Moody and Osis with Julian's account of her own
     moribund experience and resultant mystical visions, and
     finds a remarkable correlation.

546. Bynum, Caroline. "Jesus as Mother and Abbot as Mother:
     Some Themes in Twelfth-Century Cistercian Writing."
     Harvard Theological Review, 70 (1977), 257-84.

     This study of the concept of Jesus as Mother is valuable
     also as background on its use by Julian. Bynum studies
     the Motherhood of God theme in the history of doctrine,
     concentrating on Clement of Alexandria, Anselm, and
     Julian, and avers it has implications for the theology
     of the Atonement, Incarnation, and Trinity.

547. Cabussut, André. "Une Dévotion médiévale peu connue:
     la dévotion à Jésus, nôtre mère." *Revue d'Ascese et
     Mystique*, 25 (1949), 231-45.

     This important study was one of the first to explore
     the devotion to Jesus as Mother, a major motif in Julian's
     Revelations.

548. Chambers, Percy Franklin, ed. *Juliana of Norwich: An
     Introductory Appreciation and an Interpretative
     Anthology*. London: Gollancz; New York: Harpers, 1955.

549. Colledge, E., and James Walsh. "Editing Julian of Nor-
     wich's *Revelations*: A Progress Report." *MS*, 38 (1976),
     404-27.

     The substance of this report has been incorporated
     into the authors' introduction to and text of the critical
     edition of the *Showings*, and, in part, in the modernized
     version of that edition (see 506-7).

550. Cummings, C. "God's 'Homely' Love in Julian of Norwich."
     Cistercian Studies, 13 (1978), 68-74.

     A discourse on the meaning and centrality of "homely"
     and "courteous" love in Julian's writings.

551. Dalby, Joseph. *Christian Mysticism and the Natural
     World*. London: James Clark, 1949.

     A brief but penetrating insight into Julian's thought
     is contained in pp. 74-86.

552.   Dinnis, Enid. "Julian's Bread." *NCW*, 116 (1922-3),
       605-19.

       After noting the relevance of Julian's "bread"--her
       Revelations--for today's world, Dinnis discusses the
       history of the treatise in manuscript and printed
       editions; the dangers of "free-lancing" admirers of
       Julian in quoting snippets and thus tampering with the
       integrity of her message; and the doctrine and style of
       the *Revelations*.

553.   Dorgan, Sr. Margaret. "Julian of Norwich." *Spiritual
       Life*, 22 (1976), 173-8.

       A lively introduction to Julian, with support from
       contemporary scholarship.

554.   Drake, Frederick W. "Julian of Norwich." In *Masters of
       the Spiritual Life*. London: Longmans, Green and Co.,
       1916, pp. 31-54.

       Selections from great "Masters of Devotion," intended
       to promote personal religion, with each selection pre-
       ceded by an introduction concerning the text and its
       context. The section on Julian places her firmly in the
       mystic camp.

555.   Dreyer, E. "Julian of Norwich: Her Merry Counsel."
       America, 139 (1978), 55-7.

       A study of five aspects of Julian's spirituality
       which speak to the 20th century: (1) her simplicity;
       (2) her attitude toward the natural and its relation
       to the supernatural; (3) the Trinitarian dimension of
       her spirituality; (4) her use of feminine imagery; and
       (5) her vision of hope.

556.   Dulcidia, Sr. M. "Dame Julian and St. Paul." *C&C*, 7
       (1955), 100-6.

       This article adds some citations from Julian's use of
       Scripture to those noted by Anna Maria Reynolds (see
       593) and by Father Molinari (see 583). However, Molinari
       seems to be correct when he says that "Sr. Dulcidia's
       thesis is scarcely borne out by the text of the *Revela-
       tions*" (p. 191, note 1).

557.   du Moustier, Benôit. "Spiritual Childhood and Dame
       Julian of Norwich." *Pax*, 24 (1935), 281-4.

       An illuminating discussion of Chaps. 59-63 of Julian's

Revelations, concerning the Motherhood of God, with evidence of a striking parallel in the writings of Marguerite d'Oingt, Prioress of the Charterhouse of Poletine-en-Lyonnaise (d. 1310). du Moustier posits that the concept was perhaps well known among the mystical Friends of God and feels that the Motherhood of God theme is a very important part of Julian's message for us today.

558. Flinders, Carol Lee. "A Comparison of the Short and Long Text of the *Sixteen Revelations of Divine Love* by Julian of Norwich." Diss. Univ. of California, Berkeley 1972.

559. Flood, H.R. *St. Julian's Church, Norwich and Dame Julian.* Norwich: Wherry Press, 1936.

A description of St. Julian's church and a reconstruction of Julian's life as an anchoress.

560. Forbes, F.A. *Meditations on the Litany of the Sacred Heart of Jesus Culled from the Writings of Juliana of Norwich.* Preface by J.B. Jaggar. London: Burns, Oates & Washbourne, Inc., 1920, 1951; rpt. Springfield, Ill.: Templegate, 1954.

561. Foulds, Elfrida. "Mother Julian of Norwich." *Friend* (1973), pp. 581-2.

An appreciation of Julian as having value for modern-day Quakerism in her spiritual teaching. Also contains a favorable mention of Margery Kempe.

562. Graef, Hilda. "Women Mystics." In *The Light and the Rainbow.* London: Longmans; Westminster, Md.: Newman Press, 1959, pp. 242-77.

An appreciation of Julian as a mystic, showing her likeness to and difference from her contemporary, Catherine of Siena.

563. Hanshell, Deryck. "A Crux in the Interpretation of Dame Julian." *DR*, 92 (1974), 77-91.

A major article on the theology of Julian's *Revelations*. Hanshell believes Julian is primarily a theologian and, as such, orthodox in her Catholic teaching on grace and justification. He illustrates her orthodoxy by studying closely the disputed passage in which Julian states that "... in every soul that shall be

saved is a Godly will that never assented to sin, nor
ever shall." He also praises her development of the
concept of the Motherhood of Christ.

564. Haughton, Rosemary. "Five Women Who Shaped What We
Believe." *Sign*, 55 (1976), 18-23.

Julian is featured on pp. 20-1.

565. Helene, Sr. Marie. "Juliana of Norwich: Marian Mystic."
Ave Maria, 72 (1950), 335-8.

A devotional piece, more focused on devotion to Mary
than on Julian's work.

566. Israel, Martin. "A Meditation on Dame Julian's *Revelations of Divine Love*." *FCEMN*, 6/2 (1979), 66-81.

An address presented at the Julian Sexcentenary at
Norwich in 1973, extolling Julian's relevance for the
20th century.

567. James, Stanley B. "A Contemplative and the Passion."
Sign, 17 (1938), 342-4.

Popularized summary of some principal sections of
Julian's *Revelations*. James exempts Julian from the
criticism which some have leveled against recluses--
that they sought solitude to escape from worldly suf-
ferings.

568. Jewson, Charles B. *People of Medieval Norwich*. Norwich:
Jarrold, 1955.

On pp. 58-71 the essay reconstructs Julian's life in
medieval Norwich, based on historical records and the
Revelations.

569. Kroeger, Charlotte. "Die Mystikerin Lady Julian von
Norwich. Leben und Denken einer Einsidlerin aus dem
England des 14 Jahrhundert." Diss. Univ. of Hamburg,
1953.

570. Lant, Denis. "Devotional and Pastoral Classics: Mother
Julian's *Revelations of Divine Love*." *Expository
Times*, 68 (1957), 372-4.

A summary of Julian's treatise. Lant expresses some
uncomplimentary views on women mystical writers, but
excludes Julian from his criticism.

571. Lawlor, J. "A Note on the *Revelations* of Julian of
      Norwich." *RES*, N.S. 2 (1951), 255-8.

      Lawlor hypothesizes that the precedence of the Short
      Version may be because the Long Version, possibly
      extant in 1413, was not made public, owing either to
      ecclesiastic authority (an option which Lawlor prefers),
      or to Julian's "modesty and continuous quest for the
      truth," analogous to the A version of *Piers Plowman* and
      its subsequent development by Langland.

572. Levasti, Arrigo. "St. Catherine of Siena and Dame
      Julian of Norwich." Trans. Dorothy M. White." *LS*, 7
      (1953), 332-4.

      This article shows contrasts between Julian and
      Catherine on action and contemplation, on attitudes
      towards the Blood of Christ, and on the scope and in-
      terpretations of love, especially maternal love.

573. McLaughlin, Eleanor. "'Christ My Mother': Feminine
      Naming and Metaphor in Medieval Spirituality."
      Nashotah Review, 15 (1975), 229-48.

      A study of female naming of God within the Catholic
      tradition. McLaughlin discusses maternal naming of God
      in the works of the Monk of Farne, Marguerite d'Oingt
      (a 13th-century Carthusian nun), and Mechthild of
      Magdeburg (a nun of Helfta), and in a broad stream of
      other medieval writings. All of this female naming is
      for the first time, according to McLaughlin, "given
      theological context in Julian of Norwich's work of
      spiritual autobiography and direction." For a related
      study, see McLaughlin's "Les Femmes et l'hérésie
      médiévale. Un problème dans l'histoire de la spiritu-
      alité." *Concilium*, 3 (1976), 73-90.

574. Madaleva, Sr. Mary. "Dame Julian of Norwich." In
      The Image of the Work: Essays in Criticism. Ed. B.H.
      Lehman. Berkeley and Los Angeles: Univ. of California
      Press, 1955, pp. 21-32.

      A down-to-earth introduction to Julian and her *Revela-
      tions*, with historical background.

575. Maisonneuve, Roland. "L'Univers visionnaire de Julian
      of Norwich." Diss. Sorbonne Univ. 1978.

      Analyzes the *Revelations* within the formal and spiri-
      tual framework of Christian vision literature; studies

Julian's use of hyperbole, paradox, and symbolism to
manifest her beholding of God; and finds a musical dia-
lectic in the *Revelations*, used to awaken the soul to
the depths of the divine. A profound, fresh approach
to the structure and meaning of the *Revelations*. An
abstract appears in *FCEMN*, 5/3 (1979), 62-7.

576. Marshall, D.E. "St. Thomas Aquinas and Mother Julian
     on Charity." *LS*, 7 (1953), 335-41.

     There is a basic accord in the teachings of Julian
     and St. Thomas on divine charity, according to Marshall,
     but the "lyrical, passionate writing of Julian" differs
     from "the impersonal, remote style of St. Thomas."

577. Maw, M.B. "Buddhist Mysticism. A Study Based upon a
     Comparison with the Mysticism of St. Theresa and
     Juliana of Norwich." Diss. Univ. of Bordeaux 1924.

     See pp. 203-26 for an interpretation of the *Revela-
     tions*.

578. Maycock, Hugh. "Julian of Norwich." *New Fire* (1973),
     pp. 228-33.

     A comparison of Julian's ideas with those of John
     Hick and Teilhard de Chardin.

579. Meany, Mary Frances Walsh. "The Image of Christ in *The
     Revelations of Divine Love* of Julian of Norwich."
     Diss. Fordham Univ. 1975.

     Places Julian's image of Christ in the historical con-
     text of 14th-century English spirituality, and shows how
     Julian's conception of Christ corresponds to and varies
     from popular images of that milieu. The Passion is the
     dominant theme of Julian as well as of all late medieval
     piety; but Julian's most important characteristic is
     her "insistent and essential" orientation of the Passion
     to the Resurrection, an emphasis not always found in
     14th-century popular religion.

580. Members of Julian's Shrine. *Enfolded in Love: Daily
     Readings with Julian of Norwich*. London: Darton,
     Longman & Todd, 1980.

     A series of readings from Julian's *Revelations*, ar-
     ranged under subject headings for daily use over a
     period of two months.

581. Menzies, Lucy. *Mirrors of the Holy: Ten Studies in*
      Sanctity. London: A.R. Mowbray and Son, Ltd.; Mil-
      waukee: Morehouse Publishing Co., 1928.

      A book of popular piety, including an account of
      Julian.

582. Moffett, John. "God as Mother in Hinduism and Chris-
      tianity." *Cross Currents,* 27 (1978), 129-33.

      An exploration of the concept of God's Motherhood in
      the spirituality of Ramakrishna Paramahamsa and Julian
      of Norwich, in the light of Rahner's theory about the
      difference between the "word-revelation" of God and his
      "revelation through grace," and as an argument for in-
      terreligious ecumenism.

583. Molinari, Paul. *Julian of Norwich: The Teaching of a*
      Fourteenth Century English Mystic. London: Longmans,
      Green & Co., 1958.

      Subjecting Julian's *Revelations* and her personality as
      revealed therein to serious theological scrutiny,
      Molinari concludes that her mystical experiences were
      genuine and her personality, sound. He also endorses
      the orthodoxy of her teachings, from the norm of
      Catholic theology. An excellent study.

584. ————. "Love Was His Meaning: Julian of Norwich, Six
      Centuries Later." *FCEMN,* 5/4 (1979), 12-33.

      An address presented at the Julian Sexcentenary in
      Norwich, 1973, pointing to important and timely topics
      in the *Revelations*: the establishment of the identity
      of man; God's love expressed in creation and Christ's
      Passion; the centrality of the Lord/servant parable; and
      the Motherhood of God.

585. O'Donoghue, Noel D. "Visions and System: The Contribu-
      tion of the Mystical Tradition to Understanding God."
      Irish Theological Quarterly, 44 (1977) 90-104.

      Julian's concept of God is discussed on pp. 93-8.

586. Paul, Sr. Mary. *All Shall Be Well.* Fairacres, Oxford:
      S.L.G. Press, 1976.

      Subtitled "Julian of Norwich and the Compassion of
      God," this pamphlet is an in-depth approach to Julian's
      concept that "All shall be well" and to the Motherhood

of Christ sections of the *Revelations*. The author
finds in Julian echoes of the primitive Judeo-Christian
tradition of the "Holy-Spirit, the Mother," as developed,
for example, in Gregory of Nyssa.

586a. Peloquin, Sr. Carol Marie. "All Will Be Well: A Look
at Sin in Juliana's *Revelations*." *Contemplative Re-view*, 13 (1980), 9-16.

A commentary on the *Revelations*, centering around
Julian's relationship to the Trinity, and how she faces
the problem of sin.

587. Pelphrey, Charles Brant. "Julian of Norwich: A Theo-logical Reappraisal." Diss. Univ. of Edinburgh 1978.

A comprehensive, ground-breaking study of Julian.
Pelphrey sees her theology as presenting a significant
challenge to Neoplatonic thought. Her theology is
highly original, in fact, strongly resembling Byzantine
mystical theology and Orthodox thought as a whole.
An abstract appeared in *FCEMN*, 3/4 (1977), 17-18.

588. ————. "'Uncreated Charity': The Trinity in Julian
of Norwich." *Sobornost*, Series 7, No. 7 (1978), 527-35.

An important assessment of Julian's theology, holding
that Julian appears to have challenged Neoplatonism
directly, and to have taken a position different from
several key elements in the scholastic theology which
was contemporary to her. Her *Revelations* contain a
summary of Orthodox concepts, especially concerning the
Trinity. Further, she develops an ontological position
on divine love and therefore on sin and salvation.

589. Pepler, Conrad. "The Soul of a Mystic." *LS*, 3 and 4
(1949), 56-64.

Defends Julian's orthodoxy in her teaching regarding
"a Godly will that never assented to sin," even in those
who turn from God for a time. Pepler relates Julian's
teaching closely to parallels in St. Thomas and St.
Augustine.

590. ————. "The Ground of Union." *LS*, 3 and 4 (1949),
249-55.

Pepler holds that the ground of the full Christian
life of union is the faith, which "grows up into the

infused contemplation of the unitive way." He illustrates his thesis with examples from Julian.

591. ————. "The Soul of Christ." *LS*, 4 (1949), 149-56.

A summary of the doctrine on the individual soul and
Christ's soul, as the teaching relates to Julian's
Revelations.

592. Pohl, F.M. "The House of the Spirit: Mother Julian of
Norwich." *Pax*, 22 (1932-3), 108-12.

A study of Julian as the exemplar of the solitary
life, with its sorrows and joys, both in her own age
and today.

593. Reynolds, Sr. Anna Maria. "Some Literary Influences in
the *Revelations* of Julian of Norwich." In *Leeds
Studies in English and Kindred Languages*, 7-8 (1952),
18-28; rpt. Horsforth, Leeds; Trinity and All Saints'
College, 1973.

Reynolds holds that the *Revelations* has little in common with the works of Hilton, Rolle, and the *Cloud*
author, and no affinities with *The Booke of Margery
Kempe*. The influences ascribed by Reynolds are the
Bible, patristic writings, numerous echoes of Ps.-
Dionysian thought, early and contemporary English
writers (in form), especially the *Ancrene Riwle*, to which
Julian shows a similarity of spirit. But Reynolds contends that there is little trace of English formative
influence, and that the *Revelations* differ "strikingly
in important respects from contemporary religious
treatises." She shows few points of contact with contemporary women mystics, but sees possible foreign influences from Ruysbroeck, Tauler, Suso, and Eckhart.

594. ————. "Julian of Norwich." *Month*, 24 (1960), 133-44.

An important "revelation" of Julian's theology by one
of the leading Julian scholars.

595. ————. "Love is His Meaning." *CR*, 58 (1973), 363-9.

Testimony to the "serene and joyful optimism" of
Julian's spirituality.

596. ————. "'Courtesy' and 'Homeliness' in the *Revelations*
of Julian of Norwich." *FCEMN*, 5/2 (1979), 12-20.

An analysis of Julian's usage of these terms, in the

context of contemporary literary tradition and of her own mystical vision.

597. Ryder, Andrew. "A Note on Julian's Vision." *DR*, 96 (1978), 299-304.

Based on a careful appraisal of Julian's first account of her special revelations, Ryder concludes that her simple message of Christian optimism was not the result of an extraordinary divine revelation.

598. Sayer, Frank D., ed. *Julian and Her Norwich: Commemorative Essays and Handbook to the Exhibition "Revelations of Divine Love."* Norwich: Julian of Norwich 1973 Celebration Committee, 1973.

A collection of short papers about Julian and her background, together with a catalog of exhibition materials and a bibliography. Commemorates the observance of the 600th anniversary of Julian's *Revelations*, and gives evidence of the vitality of Julian scholarship and devotion today.

599. Sitwell, Gerard. "Julian of Norwich." *Sponsa Regis*, 32 (1960), 12-18.

Random comments in Mother Julian, not consistently based on scholarly opinion, and inclined to deprecate her theological underpinnings.

600. Steuart, R.H.J. "Mother Julian of Norwich." In *Diversity in Holiness*. New York: Sheed and Ward, 1937, pp. 3-17.

This essay, which originally appeared in *Blackfriars*, explores Julian's doctrinal content regarding sin, Divine Love, and the human condition.

601. Tanner, Norman P. "Popular Religion in Norwich with Special Reference to the Evidence of Wills, 1370-1532." Diss. Oxford Univ. 1973.

An excellent background study for Julian.

602. Taylor, V. "Catholic Mystics of the Middle Ages." *Edinburgh Review*, 184 (1896), 298-321; and *Living Age*, 212 (1897), 19-34.

An approach to the atmosphere and temperament of the mystic's life, citing English and Continental mystics and their works, with an emphasis on Mother Julian.

603. Thouless, Robert Henry. *The Lady Julian: A Psychological Study.* London: SPCK, 1924.

    A rather simplistic study of Julian from the standpoint of a modern Christian psychologist.

604. Tyrrell, George. "Juliana of Norwich." In *The Faith of Millions.* London: Longmans, Green & Co., 1901, pp. 1-39.

    A rather guarded endorsement of Julian's *Revelations* as an index of her mind's "thoughts and workings" and as inspired "preternatural utterances."

605. Vann, Gerald. "Juliana of Norwich on the 'Love-Longing' of Christ." *Month*, 140 (1932), 537-41.

    A superb Thomistic theological explanation of Julian's statement regarding Christ's thirst and love-longing, where Christ's human nature does not hope but desires all humankind as the fulfillment of His Mystical Body.

606. Walsh, James. "God's Homely Loving: St. John and Julian of Norwich on the Divine Indwelling." *Month*, N.S. 19 (1958), 164-72.

    A study of similarities between Julian's development of "God's homely loving" and St. John's doctrine of the divine indwelling in the souls of the just, illuminating Julian's consideration of Christ as our Mother, and her concept of the social and reciprocal aspects of the indwelling which constitute the Mystical Body. Walsh ends with Julian's statement regarding "the oneing of all mankind that shall be saved into the Blessed Trinity, thereby ending Christ's thirst and love-longing." He then avers that this testing of the *Revelations* on the divine word of Scripture places her "in the company of the great women teachers of the spiritual life, the Catherines and the Teresas."

607. ———. "A New Thérèse." *Month*, N.S. 20 (1958), 150-9.

    A comparison of the ideas of Julian and Thérèse of Lisieux.

608. ———. "A Note on Sexuality and Sensuality." *Way*, 15 (1972), 86-92.

    Discusses the real and developing correspondence between spiritual direction and psychological counseling for both the religious and the laity, drawing from the teachings of Walter Hilton and Julian.

609. ─────. *The Blissful Passion of Our Lord Jesus Christ.*
      Mother Julian of Norwich. Worcester: Stanbrook Abbey
      Press, 1973.

      Modernized selections from Julian's *Revelations.*

610. Ward, Maisie, ed. *The English Way.* New York: Sheed and
      Ward, 1933.

      Contains an excellent article by E.I. Watkin on Julian,
      pp. 128-58 (see 196).

611. Warrack, Grace, ed. *All Shall Be Well; Selections from*
      the Writings of the Lady Julian of Norwich, A.D. 1373.
      London: A.R. Mowbray & Co., Ltd., 1925.

      Selections are taken from Warrack's edition of the
      Revelations.

612. Watkin, E.I. *"Revelations of Divine Love."* *NCW,* 131
      (1930), 174-82.

      An excellent commentary on Julian's teaching on love,
      which Watkin presents as "powerfully apprehended ...
      widely explained ... winningly pictured."

613. Way, Robert E. *The Garden of the Beloved.* New York:
      Doubleday and Co., Inc.; and London: Sheldon Press,
      1975.

      The inspiration for this book is, in part, from
      Julian's parable of the Lord and the servant, where she
      says: "I beheld, thinking what manner of labor it might
      be that the servant should do. And then I understood
      that he should do the greatest labor and the hardest
      travail, that is, he should be a gardener." In this
      simple but profound allegory, Way tells a story which
      climaxes in a Disciple of Love finding the Beloved and
      becoming, in turn, a Lover who can lead a new Disciple
      through the mystic way. This is a book of great beauty
      and significance.

614. Webb, Geoffrey. "The Person and the Place--II: At Old
      St. Julian's." *LS,* 15 (1961), 549-54.

      A realistic portrait of Margery Kempe, amplified by
      what is revealed about Julian as a spiritual guide in
      Margery's report of their conversations. Webb notes a
      parallel between Julian and William Langland.

615. Webster, Alan. "Julian of Norwich." *Expository Times*, 84 (1973), 228-30.

A summary of Julian's life and concepts, which stresses her appeal to Christians, humanists, and adherents to Eastern religions.

615a. ———, ed. *Julian of Norwich: A Light in the Darkness*. London: Lawrence Rivington, 1980.

Three essays on Julian, her teachings, and her import for today's world, along with The Reverend Graham Dowell's *Julian of Norwich Dialogue* and several hymns honoring Julian. Compiled for Julian's May 8, 1980 entrance into the Calendar of the Anglican Church.

616. Windeatt, B.A. "Julian of Norwich and Her Audience." *RES*, N.S. 28 (1977), 1-17.

By comparing the prior Short Version in MS. B.L. Add. 37790 with the Long Version in MS. B.L. Sloane 2499, Windeatt shows "the mystic's development from the newness and insecurity of her position at the time of writing the Short Version towards the meditative assurances of the Long Version." In exploring the two-version manuscript tradition of the *Revelations*, Windeatt delineates "how in a person of rare sensibility, spiritual understanding and its literary expression have developed."

617. Wolters, Clifton. "Julian of Norwich Commemorative Celebration, 1373-1973." *Ampleforth Journal*, 78 (1973), 57-67.

A report on the 1973 Julian Sexcentenary at Norwich, with its goal of showing how Julian serves as a "springboard for contemporary spirituality."

618. ———. "Two Spiritualities: A Superficial Survey." *FCEMN*, 5/3 (1979), 16-27.

An address presented at the 1973 Julian Sexcentenary at Norwich, stressing the relevance of Julian's message for today's Christian spirituality, especially her emphasis on God's love for his creation, and her openness to God and the Church.

619. Zettler, Howard George. "Word Order in Late Middle English: An Analysis of the *Revelations of Divine*

Love." Diss. Univ. of Ohio 1971.

Argues that the *Revelations* reveals in late 14th-century practice and in Julian, the presence of "unconscious pressures toward the analytic, and the reduction of word-order options so strong as to dominate opposing pressures towards the synthetic and the preservation of older patterns and idioms."

VI. MARGERY KEMPE

Margery Kempe of Lynn is the most controversial of the 14th-century English mystics:
controversial to her contemporaries and to
succeeding generations of critics because of
her enthusiastic, unconventional spirituality
and idiosyncratic mystical experiences.

This section of the bibliography will
consider:
A. Editions of *The Book of Margery Kempe*.
B. Critical Studies.

A. EDITIONS

620. Butler-Bowden, William, ed. *The Book of Margery Kempe*.
      With an introduction by R.W. Chambers. London, 1936;
      New York, 1944; London: Oxford Univ. Press, 1954.

      The text of Margery's *Book*, transcribed from a Mount
      Grace Charterhouse manuscript which had remained in the
      Butler-Bowden family until 1933, when Hope Emily Allen
      identified it as the *Book*. The introduction presents
      an unsympathetic view of Margery, and, moreover, stresses
      the historical importance of the work, rather than
      Margery's spirituality.

621. Kempe, Margery. *Here begynneth a shorte treatyse of
      contemplacyon taught by our Lorde Jhesu Cryste / or
      taken out of the boke of Margerie Kempe of Lyn*.
      London: Wynkyn de Worde, 1501 (STC 14924).

      This extract from the *Book* was the only record of
      Margery Kempe until 1933.

622. Meech, Sanford B., and Hope Emily Allen, eds. *The Book
      of Margery Kempe*. EETS O.S. 212. London, 1940;
      London: Oxford Univ. Press, 1961.

      Critical text with introduction by Prof. Meech, prefa-

tory note by Hope Emily Allen, and notes and appendices
by Meech and Allen. Of special interest are Ms. Allen's
comments on "Continental Women Mystics" in the Appendix
(see 717).

B. CRITICAL STUDIES

623. Atkinson, Clarissa W. "'This Creature': A Study of *The
      Book of Margery Kempe*." Diss. Boston Univ. 1979.

      An *apologia* for Margery's orthodoxy, based on her ad-
      herence to the tradition of affective, Christocentric
      piety manifested by the Continental women mystics, and
      by such authorities as Anselm, Aelred of Rievaulx, and
      Richard Rolle. Atkinson also views the *Book* as an early
      and important source of women's history.

624. A Benedictine of Stanbrook. "Margery Kempe and the Holy
      Eucharist." *DR*, 56 (1938), 468-82.

      Concentrates on Margery's Book as evidence of the
      centrality of the Blessed Sacrament in Margery's life,
      and also as a speculum for Eucharistic devotions and
      rites in 15th-century England. In his discussion of
      Margery, the author avoids the controversy as to whether
      she is a genuine mystic or a fanatic.

625. Bennett, Henry S. "Margery Kempe." In *Six Medieval Men
      and Women*. Cambridge: Cambridge Univ. Press, 1955;
      rpt. New York: Athenaeum, 1962, pp. 124-50.

      A discourse on the *Book*, supplementing Margery's
      narrative *lacunae* regarding her trip to the Holy Land
      with a contemporary account by Friar Felix Fabri.
      Bennett also discusses her orthodoxy, in the face of
      repeated charges of Lollardry, her last pilgrimage to
      Danzig, and the scribal problems surrounding the *Book*.

626. Berry, Sara Lou. "Religious Imagery in *The Book of
      Margery Kempe*." Diss. Univ. of Florida 1962.

      An assessment of religious imagery in the *Book*, es-
      pecially regarding spiritual marriage symbolism, and of
      the language of Margery's visions and revelations.

627. Bosse, Roberta Bux. "Margery Kempe's Tarnished Reputa-
      tion: A Reassessment." *FCEMN*, 5/1 (1979), 9-19.

Argues against the generic classification of auto-
biography assigned to Margery's *Book*, and suggests that
Margery's model was the saint's life, a well-known genre
in the Middle Ages.

628. Bradford, Clara M. "Julian of Norwich and Margery
Kempe." *Theology Today*, 35 (1978), 153-8.

Contrasts two ways of describing religious experience
by citing the accounts of Julian and Margery, and adopts
the long-standing unsympathetic attitude towards Margery
in assessing her motives and character.

629. Burns, George. "Margery Kempe Reviewed." *Month*, 171
(1938), 238-44.

An excellent survey of approximately 80 reviews from
Catholic and non-Catholic critics, with Burns offering
three summary observations: (1) None of the writers
correctly analyzed Margery's "gift of tears," an ac-
credited devotion; (2) Margery's use of homely metaphors
to describe spiritual facts is characteristically
English; and (3) the *Book* illustrates the reconciliation
of the literary spirit and the spirit of prayer, with
the spiritual part taking precedence over the literary
and historical value of the *Book*.

630. Cholmeley, Katharine. *Margery Kempe, Genius and Mystic*.
London and New York: Longmans, Green, & Co., 1947.

A somewhat flowery treatment of Margery's book as a
speculum of her times, coupled with an *apologia* for her
sincerity and holiness.

631. Coleman, Thomas W. "Margery Kempe: Medieval Mystic,
Evangelist, and Pilgrim." *LQHR*, 162 (1937), 498-502.

A sympathetic treatment of Margery Kempe, attesting
to her sincerity, psychical powers, sanctity, and
humanity.

632. Colledge, E. "Margery Kempe." *Month*, 28 (1962), 16-29.

A defense of Margery Kempe, along with background
material on her life.

633. Collis, Louise. *Memoirs of a Medieval Woman. The Life
and Times of Margery Kempe*. New York: Crowell, 1964.

Formerly entitled *The Apprentice Saint*, this work is
a recreation of Margery's life and times, following the

events in her *Book*, and ending with a discussion of how
and why she wrote it.

634. Delaney, Sheila. "Sexual Economics, Chaucer's Wife of
      Bath, and *The Book of Margery Kempe*." *Minnesota Re-
      view*, N.S. 5 (1975), 104-15.

      A sociological and psychoanalytical study of Chaucer's
      Wife of Bath and Margery Kempe, as women oppressed by
      their medieval milieux. Delaney does little justice
      to the reality and sincerity of Margery's mystical ex-
      periences.

635. Goulianos, Joan, ed. *By a Woman Writt*. Baltimore:
      Penguin Books, 1974.

      Contains comments on Margery Kempe in the introduction,
      together with a short, sympathetic account of her life
      and book, and followed by a substantial excerpt from
      her work.

636. Hadshar, Albert. "Margery Kempe: Her Days and Ours."
      LS, 1 (1947), 250-7.

      An account of Margery's life and times, with an
      apologia for her holiness and an interesting history
      of her *Book*.

637. Hirsh, John C. "Author and Scribe in *The Book of Margery
      Kempe*." *MA*, 44 (1975), 245-50.

      A clear, concise exposition of the differing charac-
      teristics of the scribes and the active relation between
      author and scribe. Concludes that the "second scribe,
      no less than Margery, should be regarded as the author."

638. Mann, Henry C. "Margery Kempe." *Pax*, 26 (1937), 257-60;
      276-9.

      A strong *apologia* for Margery as a sincere and devout
      English mystic, drawing parallels with Angelo of Foligno,
      John of the Cross, and others.

639. Mason, Mary Grimley, and Carol Hurd Green. *Journals:
      Autobiographical Writings by Women*. Boston: G.K.
      Hall and Co., 1979.

      Selections from Julian and from Margery Kempe are
      included in this collection, as representatives of
      medieval women.

640. O'Connell, John R. "Mistress Margery Kempe of Lynn."
     DR, 55 (1937), 174-82.

     Taking a cautious view of Margery's mysticism,
     O'Connell states that the primary worth of Margery's
     Book resides in the fact that it is the first conscious
     and deliberate autobiography in the English language.

641. Reszkiewicz, Alfred. *Main Sentence Elements in The*
     Book of Margery Kempe. Wrockaw-Warszawa-Kraków:
     Zaklad Naradowy Imienia Ossolínskich Wydawnictwo
     Polskiej Academii Nauk, 1962.

     A structuralist analysis of the major syntax of the
     Book via a simplified system of terms and symbols which
     may be utilized for English texts of other periods.

642. Riquetti, Susanne. "A Stylistic Analysis of *The Book*
     of Margery Kempe." Diss. Oklahoma State Univ. 1978.

     A comparative analysis of the stylistic elements in
     the *Book*, centering on the rhetorical device of simile,
     repetition, and negation, and concluding that "Margery's
     illiteracy did not prevent her from assimilating that
     characteristic style of medieval mystical writing."

643. Shibata, S. "Notes on the Vocabulary of *The Book of*
     Margery Kempe." In *Studies in English Grammar and*
     Linguistics: A Miscellany in Honor of Takanobu Otsuka.
     Tokyo: Kenkysha, 1958, pp. 209-20.

644. Thornton, Martin. *Margery Kempe: An Example in the*
     English Pastoral Tradition. London: SPCK, 1960.

     The thesis of this book is that Margery Kempe should
     be considered as a "first-class parishioner," and her
     book should be considered as an ascetic and pastoral,
     rather than a mystical, treatise.

645. Thurston, Herbert. "Margery the Astonishing: A Fifteenth-
     Century English Mystic." *Month*, 24 (1936), 446-56.

     Treats Margery Kempe as one of the "queer mystics,"
     who combine "pronounced hysteria with a genuine love of
     God, great generosity and self-sacrifice, unflinching
     courage," and also who often are subject to the occur-
     rence of strange psychic phenomena.

646. Undset, Sigrid. "Margery Kempe of Lynn." *Atlantic*
     Monthly, 164 (1939), 232-40.

     A running, albeit appreciative, paraphrase of the *Book*.

647. Watkin, E.I. "In Defense of Margery Kempe." *DR*, 69
      (1941), 243-63.

      Presents a strong, persuasive defense of Margery's
      sincerity, holiness, and spirituality, and cites her
      supporters, including Julian, among those conversant
      with the contemplative life (see 196).

VII. SECONDARY WORKS, TRANSLATIONS, AND COMPILATIONS

In the past, the major critical interest has been focussed on the five leading English mystics, but more recently scholars have been examining other, lesser-known writers and mystical texts. This latter extensive corpus consists of works written in English and Latin, translations of texts composed in Latin or another foreign language, both on the Continent and in England, and compilations of mystical and devotional works.

This section of the bibliography is organized as follows:
A. Secondary Works in English and Latin.
B. English translations: Process and Works.
C. Compilations.

In all the above categories, works will be listed alphabetically by title, with editions of individual works preceding critical studies.

A. SECONDARY WORKS IN ENGLISH AND LATIN

The Cleansing of Man's Soul

648. Regan, Charles L. *"The Cleansing of Man's Soul."* Diss. Harvard Univ. 1963.

An edition, based on MS. Bodl. 923, with introduction, notes, and glossary.

649. Kirchberger, Clare. *"The Cleansing of Man's Soul." LS*, 4 (1949), 290-5.

A discussion of this penitential treatise, which is

linked to the *Chastising of God's Children*, and, in its
statements regarding reforming the soul, similar to
Hilton's *Scale*. Kirchberger also supplies a modern
English translation of the mystical portions of the
work.

Contemplations of the Dread and Love of God (H 2, pp. 73-105)

650. *Contemplacyons of the Drede and Loue of God.* London:
      Wynkyn de Worde, 1506 (STC 21259); 1520 (STC 21260).

      An early edition, erroneously attributed to Richard
      Rolle.

651. Annunziata, Anthony, ed. "*Contemplations of the Dread
      and Love of God.*" Diss. New York Univ. 1966.

      An edition based on MS. Morgan 861.

652. Comper, Frances M.M., ed. *Contemplations of the Dread
      and Love of God.* London: T. & T. Washbourne, Ltd.;
      New York: Benziger Bros., 1916.

      A Modern English version, based on MS. B.L. Harl.
      2409.

653. Krochalis, Jeanne. "*Contemplations of the Dread and
      Love of God*: Two Newly Identified Pennsylvania Manu-
      scripts." *University of Pennsylvania Library
      Chronicle*, 42 (1977), 3-22.

      A study of the manuscript tradition of this work, and
      an edition of two heretofore unreported manuscripts at
      the University of Pennsylvania Library.

The Desert of Religion: This allegorical poem, largely a
summary of virtues and vices, concerns the progressive
spiritual life to be followed by religious and lay
persons, and concludes with the contemplative life.

654. Hübner, Walter. "*The Desert of Religion.*" *Archiv*, 126
      (1911), 58-74.

      An edition of the poem, based on three B.L. manu-
      scripts: Add. 37049, Cotton Faustina B. VI, Stowe 39.
      See pp. 360-4 for a discussion by Hübner and K. Schreiner
      on the manuscripts, dialect, and sources of the poem.

655. Allen, Hope Emily. "*The Desert of Religion*: Addendum."
     Archiv, 127 (1911), 338-90.

     Points to the *Speculum Vitae* as a major source of the
     Desert.

*A Devout Treatise Called the Tree & XII Fruits of the
    Holy Ghost*

656. Vaisser, J.J., ed. *A Devout Treatyse Called the Tree
     & XII Frutes of the Holy Ghost*. Groningen: J.R.
     Walters, 1960.

     A critical edition, using MS. Fitzwilliam Museum,
     Cambridge, McClean 132 as the base text, collated with
     other manuscripts and the printed edition of 1534/5,
     with an extensive introduction on authorship, style,
     sources, and content. The work, written for a nun,
     constitutes a guide for life, with some emphasis on the
     mystical way.

*Meditaciones Ciusdam Monachi Apud Farneland Quondam
    Solitarii*: Despite the rising demand for vernacular texts,
    Latin continued to be considered as the more appropriate
    language for clerics, as evinced by Richard Methley's
    translating the *Cloud* and the "M.N." version of the
    Mirror of Simple Souls into Latin, the Carmelite Thomas
    Fishlake's Latin version of both books of *The Scale of
    Perfection*, Methley's own *Scola Amoris Languidi*, *Dormitorium
    Dilecti Dilecti*, *Refectorium Salutis*, and *Experimentum
    Veritatis* on the spiritual and contemplative life, and the
    Latin meditations of John Whiterig, the Monk of Farne, a
    14th-century Benedictine monk of Durham.

657. Farmer, Hugh. "*Meditaciones Cuiusdam Monachi Apud
     Farneland Quondam Solitarii*." *Studia Anselmiana*,
     41 (1957), 141-245.

     The first printing of these Latin *Meditations*. The
     introduction includes a study of the historical back-
     ground as well as a summary and analysis of the *Medita-
     tions*. Farmer finds the Monk of Farne "more calm, more
     Scriptural, and theological" than Rolle, although
     Whiterig resembles Rolle in some ways.

658. ———. *The Monk of Farne*. Baltimore: Helicon Press,
     1961.

     A Modern English translation of six selections, which

reveal not only the monastic milieu which informed the
author, but also his personal spirituality. In addition
there is an excellent bibliography and critical notes,
and an extensive introduction on the English mystical
tradition and on the relevance of that tradition to
today's world.

659. Pantin, William A. "The Monk-Solitary of Farne: A
      Fourteenth-Century English Mystic." *English His-
      torical Review*, 59 (1944), 162-86.

      A thorough study that places the Monk of Farne not
      only in the mainstream of medieval mysticism, but more
      specifically as a link between the schools of Anselm and
      Bernard and the classical 14th-century mystics.

Speculum Vitae: This work of 8,000 rimed couplets has been
      ascribed to William of Nassington, along with a metrical
      version of Rolle's *Form of Living* (H 2, pp. 282-92),
      *St. Mary's Lamentation to St. Bernard on the Passion of
      Christ* (H 2, pp. 274-82), and *Tractatus de Trinitate et
      Unitate* (H 2, pp. 334-9).

660. Smeltz, John W. "*Speculum Vitae*: An Edition of MS.
      B.L. Royal 17 C. viii." Diss. Duquesne Univ. 1977.

      An exploration of the earlier traditions and sources
      of the *Speculum Vitae*, an analysis of the content and
      structure of the work, and an edition of the complete
      text.

661. Gunn, Agnes. "Accidia and Prowess in the Vernon Version
      of Nassyngton's *Speculum Vitae*: An Edition of the
      Text and a Study of the Ideas." Diss. University
      of Pennsylvania 1969.

      Deals with the 4,000-line fragment of the poem con-
      tained in the Vernon manuscript.

662. Nelson, Venetia C. "An Introduction to the *Speculum
      Vitae*." *Essays in Literature* (Denver), 2 (1974),
      75-102.

      A comparison of the *Speculum Vitae* with its prose
      version, *The Mirror of Life*, in MS. B.L. Harl. 45,
      and a close examination of the *Speculum*.

663. ———. "The Vernon and Simeon Copies of the *Speculum
      Vitae*." *English Studies*, 57 (1976), 390-4.

A study of the manuscript tradition of the *Speculum Vitae*, concluding that the Simeon text was copied from the Vernon, and that, for the *Speculum* at least, Simeon postdates Vernon.

664. ———. "Problems of Transcription in the *Speculum Vitae* Manuscripts." *Scriptorium*, 31 (1977), 254-9.

A discussion of the paleographic problems entailed in transcribing manuscripts of the *Speculum*, owing to the scribes' varying use of otiose strokes and unusual abbreviations, along with some graphemic confusion.

665. ———. "Cotton Tiberius E. VII: A Manuscript of the *Speculum Vitae*." *English Studies*, 59 (1978), 97-113.

A careful study of the scribal practices of commonplace variation and radical alteration in this unique version of the *Speculum*.

666. Stover, Edna V. "*A Myrrour to Lewde Men and Wymmen*." Diss. Univ. of Pennsylvania 1951.

An edition of the prose *Mirror*, drawn from the University of Pennsylvania manuscript.

667. ———. "*A Myrrour to Lewde Men and Wymmen*: A Note on a Recently Acquired Manuscript." *University of Pennsylvania Library Chronicle*, 16 (1950), 81-6.

A report on a new manuscript of this prose work, which Stover avers is derived from the *Speculum Vitae*.

A Talking of the Love of God (H 2, pp. 345-66; see also 224-5, 233-4)

668. Westra, M. Salvina. *A Talking of the Love of God*. The Hague: M. Nijhoff, 1950.

A critical edition from MS. Vernon, collated with MS. Simeon, with facing Modern English translation. The introductory analysis of the text, its method of composition, and imputed author and audience is somewhat confusing; the section on phonology and grammar is extensive.

669. Konrath, M. "Eine übersehene Fassung der *Ureisun of Ure Lauerde*, bez. *Ureisun of God Almihti* und der

Wohunge of Ure Lauerde." *Anglia*, 42 (1918), 85-98.

A discussion of *A Talking of the Love of God* as an amalgam of borrowings, the first part from the *Ureisum of Ure Lauerde* and the last part from the *Wohunge*. Also considers the "Cadence ... riht poynted" form of the work, and imputes an audience of women religious.

670. Thompson, Meredith, ed. Þe *Wohunge of Ure Lauerd and Other Pieces.* EETS O.S. 241. London: Oxford Univ. Press, 1958 (for 1955); rpt. with corrections, 1970.

A critical edition of the Wooing Group, based on MS. B.L. Cotton Titus D. XVIII, with an excellent introduction discussing origin and literary relationships, form and style, and the importance of this corpus for later mystical writings in England, especially *A Talking of the Love of God*.

671. Vollhardt, William. *Einfluss der lateinischen geistlichen Literatur auf einige Schöpfungen der englischen Übergangsperiode.* Leipzig: Hesse und Becker, 1888.

Stresses the predominant informing influence of medieval Latin devotional literature, rather than vernacular writings, on the Wooing Group.

To Hew Heremyte A Pystyl of Solitary Lyfe Nowadayes

672. Hogg, James, ed. *Richard Methley: To Hew Heremyte A Pystyl of Solytary Lyfe Nowadayes.* Analecta Cartusiana 31. Salzburg, 1977, pp. 91-119.

A critical edition of the text, with an extensive and informative introduction on Richard Methley, his milieu, and his work. A modernized text, "*An Epistle of Solitary Life*," with an introduction by W.E. Campbell, is contained in *The Thought and Culture of the English Renaissance: An Anthology of Tudor Prose*, ed. Elizabeth Nugent. Cambridge, 1956, pp. 387-93.

B. ENGLISH TRANSLATIONS: PROCESS AND WORKS

B1. ENGLISH TRANSLATIONS: PROCESS: Although devotional works
continued to be written in or translated into Latin,
presumably for clerics, the increasing demand for vernacular texts on the part of lay and religious audiences
resulted in a large number of translations. These translations were accomplished to a great extent by members
of religious orders.

673. Clay, Rotha M. "Further Studies on Medieval Recluses."
      British Archaeological Association, 16 (1953), 74-86.

      A supplement to *The Hermits and Anchorites of England*
      (see 151) concerning literary recluses such as John
      Lacy at Blackfriars, Newcastle-on-Tyne, the Carthusian
      John Dygoun of Sheen, and Simon Appulby of London Wall.
      Of interest in showing the recluses' dedication to
      their literary, devotional tasks.

674. Pepler, Conrad. "John Lacy: A Dominican Contemplative."
      LS, 5 (1951), 397-400.

      Outlines Lacy's literary and scribal activities.

675. Power, Eileen. *Medieval English Nunneries, c. 1275-
      1535*. Cambridge: Cambridge Univ. Press, 1922.

      An important study, with Chap. 6, "Education," pp.
      236-84, illustrating the practices and necessity for
      translating texts into English for the women religious.

      As the following studies elucidate, by far
      the major impetus for the writing, editing,
      translation, and transmission of mystical
      texts can be credited to the Carthusian
      Charterhouse at London, Sheen, and Mount Grace,
      and individuals such as John Grenehalgh and
      Nicholas Love; and to the Bridgettine (Bir-
      gittine) community at Syon Abbey, one of the
      most prestigious religious houses in England,
      from its founding in 1415 until the Dissolu-
      tion.

676. Bateson, Mary, ed. *Catalogue of the Library of Syon
      Monastery, Isleworth*. Cambridge: Cambridge Univ.
      Press, 1898.

      Catalogue of Syon Library, contained in MS. Corpus

Christi 141, including manuscripts and printed books,
with an introductory assessment of the library in the
light of Syon's history.

677. Blunt, John H., ed. *The Myroure of Oure Ladye*. EETS
      E.S. 19. London: N. Trübner & Co., 1873.

      A compilation of the Hours and Masses of the Virgin,
      prepared for the Sisters of Syon. It is interesting to
      note that the compiler drew on Rolle for the authorized
      English text of the Psalms.

678. Colledge, E. "*Epistola Solitarii ad Reges*: Alphonse
      of Pecha as Organizer of Birgittine and Urbanist
      Propaganda." *MS*, 17 (1956), 19-49.

      A clear, detailed history of St. Bridget's life and
      Revelations, the cause of her canonization, and the
      central role played by Alphonse of Pecha in these ac-
      tivities. Colledge's notes provide valuable biblio-
      graphic information on St. Bridget and her Order.
      (Note: Chaps. 19-20 of the *Chastising of God's
      Children* [see 694-702] were taken from the *Epistola*.)

679. ————. "A Syon Centenary." *LS*, 15 (1961), 308-16.

      A brief history of the Bridgettine community at Syon.
      (Note: This has been reprinted as a pamphlet distributed
      by Syon Abbey, located today at South Brent, Devon,
      England.)

680. Collins, A. Jeffries. *The Bridgettine Breviary of Syon
      Abbey*. Henry Bradshaw Society. Worcester: Stanbrook
      Abbey Press, 1969.

      The text of the Breviary, drawn from MS. Magdalene
      College, Cambridge F.4.11

681. *A History of the County of Middlesex*. Eds. J.S. Cock-
      burn, H.P.F. King, and K.G.T. McConnell. London:
      Oxford Univ. Press, 1969, I, 182-91.

      F.R. Johnston's discussion of Syon Abbey and a survey
      of devotional texts produced at Syon in the late 15th
      and early 16th centuries.

682. Hogg, James. "Carthusian Materials in the London Public
      Record Office Collection SPI/239." *Analecta Cartusiana*,
      37 (1977), 134-44.

      Contains information concerning Richard Methley.

682a. ———. *The Rewyll of Seynt Sauiore and Other Middle English Birgittine Legislative Texts*, II. Salzburger Studien zur Anglistik und Amerikanistik 6. Salzburg, 1978.

Facsimiles of MSS. Cambridge Univ. Library Ff. 6. 33 and St. John's College, Cambridge 11 (the latter in Latin), with introductory descriptions of the manuscripts, both of which are associated with Sheen Charterhouse and Syon Abbey.

683. ———. "Unpublished Texts in the Carthusian North Middle English Religious Miscellany MS. B.L. Add. 3074." In *Essays in Honour of Erwin Stürzl on his Sixtieth Birthday*. Vol. I. Salzburg: Institut für englische Sprache und Literatur, 1980, pp. 241-84.

A careful assessment of MS. 3074 as a "witness of what a late medieval Carthusian read," along with a transcript of some of the texts.

684. Johnston, F.R. *Syon Abbey: A Short History of the English Bridgettines*. Eccles and District History Society, in association with Syon Abbey, 1964.

A monograph, presenting the medieval and ongoing history of Syon Abbey.

685. Sargent, Michael. "The Transmission by the English Carthusians of Some Late Medieval Spiritual Writings." *JEH*, 27 (1976), 225-40.

A compendious and important study of the Carthusian Order's dissemination of mystical texts, including works of Rolle, Hilton, and the Continental mystics, an endeavor which Sargent feels can be ascribed "to the literary character of the spirituality of the Carthusian Order," as outlined in the *Consuetudines* of Guido I.

685a. ———. "James Grenehalgh as Textual Critic." Diss. Univ. of Toronto 1979.

B2. ENGLISH TRANSLATIONS: WORKS

The Abbey of the Holy Ghost (H 1, pp. 321-37), taken from
L'Abbaye du Saint Esprit (also in a Latin version,
Abbacia de Sancto Spiritu), and *The Charter of the
Abbey of the Holy Ghost* (H 1, pp. 337-62)

686. Garrett, Robert Max. *The Abbey of the Holy Ghost*. New
York: T.A. Wright, 1918.

A modern edition of the text.

687. Brook, Stella. *"The Charter of the Abbey of the Holy
Ghost."* MLR, 54 (1959), 481-8.

Defends this work against its usual unfair comparison
with the *Abbey*.

688. Chesney, Kathleen. "Notes on Some Treatises of Devotion Intended for Margaret of York (MS. Douce 365)."
MA, 20 (1951), 11-39.

In her discussion of the *Abbey*, Chesney contends
that the *L'Abbaye du Saint Esprit* may be indebted to
Book III of *De Claustro Animae* for the idea of the
figurative cloister. She also finds that variants of
the French versions reflect the deliberate elaboration
of a vernacular text, not the individual renderings of
different translators.

689. Collins, A.J. "Middle English Devotional Pieces."
British Museum Quarterly, 14 (1940), 87-8.

Report on MS. Egerton 3245, which contains *The Abbey
of the Holy Ghost* and the *Charter*, along with other
works.

690. Conlee, John W. *"The Abbey of the Holy Ghost* and the
Eight Ghostly Dwelling Places of Huntington Library
HM 744." *MA*, 44 (1975), 137-44.

Examines these two works under the aspect of their
use of the metaphor of the cloister to stand for the
soul. Notes that they are the only known contributions
in Middle English to the large and varied traditions of
writings depicting a figurative cloister.

691. Consacro, Peter. "The Author of *The Abbey of the Holy
Ghost*: A Popularizer of the Mixed Life." *FCEMN*, 2/4
(1976), 15-20.

Using his unpublished edition of the MS. Vernon text,
Consacro posits that the controversy over the possibility
of the "mixed life" may have been largely academic,
since this widely disseminated work was intended for
ordinary lay people, to whom the goal of mystic union
was held out.

The Book of Ghostly Grace, from St. Mechthild of
  Hackeborn's *Liber Spiritualis Gratiae*

692. Halligan, Theresa A., ed. *The Booke of Gostlye Grace*
      of Mechthild of Hackeborn. Toronto: Pontifical In-
      stitute of Mediaeval Studies, 1979.

      The *Booke* is a Middle English text of the visions and
      revelations of the German mystic, St. Mechthild of
      Hackeborn, translated from a Latin version of the
      German original. Halligan believes the value of the
      work was rooted in its basically homiletic point of
      view, and also that it served as a handbook of devotional
      practices, even though it contains detailed, imaginative
      descriptions of the splendor of the special graces be-
      stowed as rewards for a pious life. The possibility of
      Carthusian authorship of the Middle English version is
      not unreasonable, according to Halligan.

693. ————. "The *Revelations* of St. Matilda in English:
      The Booke of Gostlye Grace." *N&Q*, N.S. 21 (1974),
      443-6.

      Gives general background on the *Booke*, and cites
      evidence linking this work to the Carthusians and Syon
      Abbey. Halligan also notes that an abridgement of the
      work circulated on the Continent as early as the mid-
      14th century.

The Chastising of God's Children and *The Treatise of*
  Perfection of the Sons of God, from Jan van Ruysbroeck's
  Die Gheestelijcke Brulocht (*The Spiritual Espousals*)
  and *Van den Blinckenden Steen* (*The Sparkling Stone*)
  respectively

694. Bazire, Joyce, and E. Colledge, eds. *The Chastising*
      of God's Children and The Treatise of Perfection of
      the Sons of God. Oxford: Basil Blackwell, 1957.

      An invaluable introduction, giving the manuscript
      tradition, dating (1382-1408), sources, cultural and

religious milieux, and doctrinal content, followed by
the critical texts and copious notes. Both the introduction and the notes place the two works in the context
of English and Continental mysticism.

695. Colledge, E., ed. and trans. *The Spiritual Espousals*.
      New York: Harper & Bros., 1953.

      A Modern English translation, with an introduction
      on Ruysbroeck's orthodox doctrine on the contemplative
      life, as presented in the *Espousals* and his other works.

696. Underhill, Evelyn, ed. *The Adornment of the Spiritual
      Marriage, The Sparkling Stone, The Book of Supreme
      Truth*. Trans. C.A. Wynschenk. Introduction and
      notes by Evelyn Underhill. London: J.M. Dent & Sons,
      Ltd.; New York: E.P. Dutton & Co., 1916.

      A Modern English translation of these three books,
      with an introduction on the thematic content of Ruys-
      broeck's mystical writings.

697. Bazire, Joyce. "The Dialects of the Manuscripts of
      The Chastising of God's Children." *English and
      Germanic Studies*, 6 (1957), 64-78.

      Through an analysis of the dialect features and
      variants of the nine manuscripts and the Wynkyn de Worde
      edition of the *Chastising*, Bazire theorizes that the
      original dialect of the author was at least partly
      Southeastern in character.

698. Bühler, Curt F. "Seven Variants in *The Chastising of
      God's Children*." *Papers of the Bibliographical
      Society of America*, 43 (1949), 75-8.

      A study of seven variants in the Wynkyn de Worde
      printed edition of the *Chastising*, pointing the way for
      further bibliophilic research on early editions of
      mystic texts.

699. Colledge, E. "*The Treatise of Perfection of the Sons
      of God*." *English Studies*, 33 (1952), 49-66.

      A study of Carthusian transmission and 15th-century
      translation of Jan van Ruysbroeck's *Die Gheestelijcke
      Brulocht* and *Van den Blinckenden Steen*, both from Latin
      translations of the original Dutch by William Jordaens.

700. De Soer, G.B. "The Relationship of the Latin Version
      of Ruysbroeck's *Die Geestelike Brulocht* to *The*

Chastising of God's Children." *MS*, 21 (1959), 129-46.

A comparative study, showing that the *Chastising* was translated from Gerard Groote's Latin version, *De Ornatu Spiritualis Disponsationis*, and not from Jordaen's *De Ornatu Spiritualium Nuptiarum*.

701. Kirchberger, Clare. "English Devotional Literature." *LS*, 4 (1949), 512-4.

Points to the need for scholarly investigation of English devotional works written during the 14th and 15th centuries, using *The Chastising of God's Children* and its component tracts as an example.

702. Sargent, Michael. "A New Manuscript of *The Chastising of God's Children*." *MA*, 46 (1977), 49-65.

A scholarly discussion of the spurious attribution to Walter Hilton of the text of the *Chastising*, contained in MS. 3084 (c. 1450) of the Walker-Heneage (Button) collection. Sargent supports his thesis with scrupulous manuscript evidence, and also posits a London Charter-house/Sheen/Syon Abbey provenance for MS. 3084.

Of the Doctrine of the Heart, attributed to Gerard of Liège's *Doctrina Cordis*

703. Candon, Sr. Mary Patrick. "An Edition of the 15th-Century Middle English Translation of Gerard of Liège's *De Doctrina Cordis*." Diss. Fordham Univ. 1963.

An edition of this tract, instructing nuns on the preparation for union with God, and stressing devotion to the Sacred Heart of Jesus.

704. Kirchberger, Clare. "Mystical Prayer." *LS*, 4 (1949), 147-8.

A modernized version of the text, *Of the Doctrine of the Heart*, from MS. Bodl. Douce 262. A fuller modernized text is contained in *The Coasts of the Country*, pp. 109-16 (see 108).

705. Wilmart, André. "Gerard de Liège: Un trait unédit de l'amour de Dieu." *Revue d'Ascetique et de Mystique*, 12 (1931), 349-430.

Formula Noviciorum, from David of Augsburg's *De Exterioris et Interioris Hominis Compositione*

706. Jolliffe, Peter S. "Middle English Translations of the *De Exterioris et Interioris Hominis Compositione*." *MS*, 36 (1974), 259-77.

A treatment of the *Formula Noviciorum*, contained in MSS. Queen's College, Cambridge 31 and Cambridge Univ. Library Dd. 233, a Syon text, as well as some shorter Middle English translations. Jolliffe stresses that these vernacular translations were increasingly intended not only for professed religious but also for devout laity.

707. David of Augsburg. *De Exterioris et Interioris Compositione Secundum Triplicem Statum Incipientium Proficientium et Perfectorum*. Quaracchi, 1899.

Critical edition, with all three books attributed to David of Augsburg.

708. ―――. *Spiritual Life and Progress*. Ed. and trans. Dominic Devas. 2 vols. London: Burns, Oates & Washbourne, 1937.

Informacio Alredi Abbatis Monasterij de Rieualle ad Sororem Suam Inclusam, from Aelred of Rievaulx's *De Institutione Inclusarum*

709. Horstmann, Carl, ed. "*Informacio Alredi Abbatis Monasterij de Rieualle ad Sororem Suam Inclusam*: Translate de Latino in Anglicum per Thomam N. (Aus MS. Vernon)." *ES*, 7 (1884), 304-44.

Thomas N's Middle English translation of Aelred's *De Institutione Inclusarum*, a guide for living directed to a recluse, and concerned with achieving the contemplative life.

710. Talbot, Charles H. "The *De Institutis Inclusarum* of Aelred of Rievaulx." *Analecta Sacri Ordinis Cisterciansis*, 7 (1951), 167-217.

An expert analysis of the influence of the *De Institutis Inclusarum*, its probable sources, its content, a list of manuscripts, and the Latin text, drawn from MS. B.L. Cotton Nero A III.

711. Webb, Geoffrey, and Adrian Walker, eds. *Aelred of
     Rievaulx. A Letter to His Sister.* London: A.R. Mow-
     bray & Co., Ltd., 1957.

A Ladder of Four Rungs, from Guigo II's *Scala Claustralium*

712. Hodgson, Phyllis. "*A Ladder of Foure Ronges by the
     Whiche Men Mowe Wele Clyme to Heaven*: A Study of the
     Prose Style of a Middle English Translation." *MLR*,
     44 (1949), 466-75.

     An important study of this 15th-century translation
     to show the excellence of the prose and the influence
     of such translations on English prose (see 394).

713. Colledge, Edmund, and James Walsh, eds. *Guiges II Le
     Chartreux: Lettre sur la Vie Contemplative (L'échelle
     des moines) Douze Meditations.* Paris: Les Editions
     du Cerf, 1970.

     Critical text of Guigo II's *Epistola de Vita Contem-
     plativa* (*Scala Claustralium*) and *Meditations,* with
     introduction and parallel French translation.

714. ———. *Guigo II. The Ladder of Monks: A Letter on the
     Contemplative Life and Twelve Meditations.* Garden
     City, N.Y.: Doubleday & Co., 1978.

     Modern English version of the editor's .critical edition,
     with a scholarly introduction.

715. A Monk of Parkminster. "Guigo the Angelic, His Works
     and Teachings." *Month,* 27 (1962), 215-26.

     An examination of Guigo II's life and spiritual works,
     especially his *Scala Claustralium.*

Lives of Women Mystics

716. Horstmann, Carl. "Prosalegenden: Die Legenden des MS.
     Douce 114." *Anglia,* 8 (1885), 102-96.

     An edition of the first four legends in MS. Douce
     114, which are Middle English translations of the lives
     of four Continental women mystics: St. Elizabeth of
     Spalbeck (d. 1266); St. Christina Mirabilis (d. 1224);
     St. Mary of Oegines (d. 1263); and St. Catherine of
     Siena (Senis), with a brief introduction by Horstmann
     concerning the manuscript, the Latin sources of the

legends, other translations, and authorship. (Note: In the Meech/Allen edition of *The Book of Margery Kempe*, pp. lxi-lxvii [see 622], Hope Emily Allen suggested a study of unedited 15th-century translations from Continental works of feminine piety, in order to adduce the influence of these writings on the native English mystical tradition.)

717. Talbot, C.H., ed. *The Life of Christina of Markyate, A Twelfth Century Recluse.* Oxford: Clarendon Press, 1959.

A Modern English translation, with facing Latin, of the life of this 12th-century recluse and visionary, drawn from MS. B.L. Cotton Tib. E. I.

The Mirror of the Church (H 1, pp. 219-61) of Edmund Rich, from his *Speculum Ecclesie* and *Merure de Seinte Eglise*

718. Forshaw, Helen P., ed. *Edmund of Abingdon's Speculum Religiosorum and Speculum Ecclesie.* Auctores Britannici Medii Aevi. Oxford: Oxford Univ. Press, 1973.

Critical edition of the Latin text.

719. Goymer, C.B. "A Parallel Text Edition of the Middle English Prose Version(s) of the *Mirror* of St. Edmund, Based on Known Complete Manuscript." M.A. Thesis Univ. of London 1962.

720. Perry, George, ed. *Religious Pieces in Prose and Verse.* EETS O.S. 26. London: H. Trübner & Co., 1889.

A collection containing *The Mirror of St. Edmund* and *The Abbey of the Holy Ghost*, which, according to Perry, show how to clothe the active life with the form and spirit of the contemplative way.

721. Rich, Edmund. *The Myrrour of the Chyrche.* London: Wynkyn de Worde, 1521 (STC 965); 1527 (STC 966).

722. ————. *The Myrour of the Chyrche.* London: Peter Treueres, n.d.

723. Robbins, Harry Wolcott. "An English Version of St. Edmund's *Speculum*. Ascribed to Richard Rolle." *PMLA*, 40 (1925), 240-51.

Presents a summary of English prose translations of Edmund Rich's *Speculum Ecclesie* (c. 1240), the majority of which are 15th century, and the text of MS. Cambridge Univ. Ii. 6. 40, which is unique in ascribing the treatise to Richard Rolle.

724. ————. *Le Merure de Seinte Eglise. An Early Example of Rhythmical Prose in the Anglo-Norman Dialect, from the MSS. at Oxford, Cambridge, London, Durham, and Paris, and Richard Rolle's Devout Meditaciones, a Partial Translation of St. Edmund's Merure into Middle English.* Lewisburg, Pa.: Univ. Print Shop, 1923.

An edition of the *Merure*, together with a preliminary accounting of the manuscripts of English provenance.

725. Steele, Francesca M., ed. *The Mirror of St. Edmund.* London: Burns & Oates, 1905.

A Modern English version of the *Mirror*.

726. Forshaw, Helen P. "New Light on the *Speculum Ecclesie* of St. Edmund of Abingdon." *Archives d'Histoire Doctrinale et Littéraire du Moyen Age*, 38 (1971), 7-33.

727. ————. "St. Edmund's *Speculum*: A Classic of Victorine Spirituality." *Archives d'Histoire Doctrinale et Littéraire du Moyen Age*, 39 (1972), 7-40.

This and the preceding study show that although the work is primarily didactic, it also treats of mysticism. Forshaw argues for the unity of the whole work, its indebtedness to Hugh of St. Victor's teaching on meditation and contemplation, and to St. Gregory the Great as the source for Chap. 29 on mysticism. She also contends that the absence of Dionysian mystical terminology may have been a factor in the work's popularity throughout the Middle Ages.

728. Legge, M. Dominica. "St. Edmund on the 'Hours.'" *MLR*, 29 (1934), 72-4.

Discusses the relationship between sections of MS. Lambeth Palace Lib. 522 and St. Edmund's *Merure de Seinte Eglise*, and concludes they both have the same author. Legge theorizes that St. Edmund wrote the shorter piece earlier and then absorbed it into the longer *Merure*.

729. ————. "Wanted--An Edition of St. Edmund's *Merure*."
      MLR, 54 (1959), 72-4.

      Posits the need for further work and a critical edi-
      tion going beyond the work done by H.W. Robbins, and
      opts for French as the original language.

730. Wilshere, Alan. "The Latin Primacy of St. Edmund's
      Mirror of the Holy Church." *MLR*, 71 (1976), 500-12.

      While there is a consensus that St. Edmund's *Mirror*
      is a seminal text in the development of English mysti-
      cism, there is no such agreement on the language of the
      original version. Basing his opinion on comparative
      studies of the lexicon, terminology, and syntax, Wil-
      shere carries forth Helen Forshaw's findings in favor
      of a Latin original.

The Mirror of Simple Souls, from Margaret Porete's
  Miroir des simple ames

731. Doiron, Marilyn. "Þe *Mirrour of Simple Soules*: An
      Edition and Commentary." Diss. Fordham Univ. 1964.

      This is the first collated edition of the three Middle
      English manuscripts. Doiron accepts the authorship of
      Margaret Porete as reasonable, and discusses the possi-
      bility of the translator being Michael of Northbrook,
      Bishop of London. She finds certain passages in the
      Mirrour which could be interpreted as heretical, but
      considers the general presentation orthodox. The presen-
      tation of the seven stages of the soul is repetitious,
      but the dialogue form redeems the work from complete
      monotony. The main idea in the *Mirrour* is the glorifica-
      tion of love above intellectual knowledge in striving
      for perfection. Its contribution to religious prose
      lies in its combining of ascetical and mystical teachings
      in the same treatise.

732. ————. "Margaret Porete: *The Mirror of Simple Souls*,
      A Middle English Translation." *AISP*, 5 (1968), 241-
      355.

      A critical edition of the Middle English text, using
      MS. St. John's College, Cambridge 71 as the base text,
      collated with MSS. B.L. Add. 37790 and Bodl. 505.

733. Guarnieri, Romana. "Il Movimento del Libero Spirito."
      AISP, 4 (1965), 351-708.

A study of the Free Spirit heresy from its origins until the 16th century, and an edition of the Old French *Miroir des simple ames*, with a discussion of the Middle English translation on pp. 508-9.

734. Kirchberger, Clare, ed. *The Mirror of Simple Souls*. London: Burns, Oates & Washbourne, Ltd., 1927.

A Modern English text, based on MS. Bodl. 505, with an extensive introduction, in which Kirchberger analyzes the form and content of the work, and disagrees with the position of Colledge, Guarnieri, and other scholars who hold that this book is essentially heretical. No mention is made of Margaret Porete, and authorship is ascribed to an unknown priest or Carthusian in the last third of the 13th century.

735. Colledge, Edmund. "Liberty of Spirit: *The Mirror of Simple Souls*." In *Theology of Renewal*, ed. L.K. Shook. New York: Herder and Herder, 1968, 100-17.

Colledge considers the *Mirror* a consciously heretical work because of its extreme Quietism and Valentian Gnosticism, and claims that "M.N." and Richard Methley, as well as others who defended its orthodoxy, were in error. In Colledge's words, "Liberty of the spirit is in truth an imprisonment in a darkness of the mind."

736. ————, and Romana Guarnieri. "The Glosses by 'M.N.' and Richard Methley to *The Mirror of Simple Souls*." *AISP*, 5 (1968), 357-82.

The glosses and emendations to the English ("M.N.") and Latin (Methley) translations of the *Mirror* are carefully assessed to illustrate the attempts of the two translators to present the *Mirror* as an orthodox mystical work, which they evidently believed, despite the heretical doctrines contained therein.

737. Doiron, Marilyn. "The Middle English Translation of *Le Mirour des Simples Ames*." In *Dr. L. Reypens-Album*. Ed. Albert Ampe. Antwerp: Uitgave Van Het Ruusbroec-Genootschap, 1964, pp. 131-52.

A comparison of the French text in MS. Chantilly 157, edited by Romana Guarnieri, and the Middle English translation by "M.N." contained in MS. St. John's College, Cambridge 71, exploring in particular the 15 additional glosses and the style of "M.N."

738. Leff, Gordon. *Heresy in the Later Middle Ages. The Relation of Heterodoxy to Dissent, c. 1250-1450.* 2 Vols. Manchester: Manchester Univ. Press; New York: Barnes & Noble, 1967.

This important work, in the author's own words, studies "the convergence between the heretical and the non-heretical." See especially I, Chap. 4, for Leff's study of the heresy of the Free Spirit.

739. Lerner, Robert. "The Image of Mixed Liquids in Late Medieval Mystical Thought." *Church History*, 40 (1971), 397-411.

A study of the significant mixed liquid imagery in the works of Jacopone da Todi, the German and Flemish mystics, and the Free Spirit heretical writers, exemplified by Margaret Porete's *Mirror of Simple Souls.*

740. ———. "The Predicament of the Mystics." In *The Heresy of the Free Spirit in the Later Middle Ages.* Berkeley: Univ. of California Press, 1972.

An enlightening study of the Free Spirit heresy, of special interest for its treatment of Margaret Porete and the *Mirror of Simple Souls* (pp. 68-78, 200-8), and also the later German and Flemish mystics (pp. 182-99).

741. McLaughlin, Eleanor. "The Heresy of the Free Spirit and Late Medieval Mysticism." *Medievalia et Humanistica*, N.S. 4 (1973), 37-54.

As a general methodological principle, McLaughlin urges that the subject of medieval heresy be approached within the context of medieval spirituality as a whole. In this regard, her treatment of the *Mirror of Simple Souls* as the "ambiguous middle ground" between orthodox spirituality and heresy puts her in conflict with Romana Guarnieri and Jean Orcibal, who, she believes, place the *Mirror* too exclusively in relation to traditional categories, the former heretical, the latter orthodox.

742. Orcibal, Jean. "*Le Miroir des Simples Ames* et le 'Secte du Libre Esprit.'" *Revue de l'Histoire des Religions*, 176 (1969), 35-60.

An argument for the orthodoxy of the *Mirror*, which Orcibal maintains should be studied in the context of orthodox mysticism, since its condemnation by the Church may have had a pastoral rather than a theological motive.

743. Underhill, Evelyn. "*The Mirror of Simple Souls.*"
      Fortnightly Review, 95 (1911), 345-54.

      Upholds the orthodoxy of the *Mirror.*

The Orchard of Syon, from the Latin translation of St.
Catherine of Siena's *Il Libro (Dialogo)*

744. Hodgson, Phyllis, and Gabriel Liegey, eds. *The
      Orcherd of Syon,* Vol. I. EETS O.S. 285. London:
      Oxford Univ. Press, 1966.

      A critical edition of the work, which is a free 15th-
      century translation of the mystical *Dialogue* of Catherine
      of Siena, written for the cloister of Syon. (Note:
      Vol. II is scheduled to contain an introduction, dis-
      cussing the work, and explanatory notes.)

745. Catherine of Siena. *Orcharde of Syon.* Trans. Dane
      James. London: Wynkyn de Worde, 1519.

746. Cavallini, Giuliana, ed. *Il Dialogo della Divina
      Providenza.* Centro Nazionale de Studi Cateriniani.
      Rome: Edizioni Cateriniane, 1968.

      A critical edition of the Italian *Dialogo,* with an
      excellent introduction and presentation of a new or-
      ganizational schema for the work.

747. Thorold, Algar, trans. *The Dialogue of the Seraphic
      Virgin Catherine of Siena.* London: Kegan Paul,
      Trench, Trübner, 1896; rpt. in abridged form by Kegan
      Paul, and Benziger in New York; reissued London:
      Burns, Oates & Washbourne; New York: Benziger, 1925.
      Further drastically abridged by Westminster, Md.:
      The Newman Bookshop, 1943.

      A Modern English translation of the *Dialogue.*

748. Ashley, Benedict. "Guide to Saint Catherine's *Dialogue.*"
      C&C, 29 (1977), 237-49.

      An analysis of the structure of the *Dialogue,* illumina-
      ting Catherine's spirituality, and suggesting its rele-
      vance for today's world.

749. Brinkworth, Guy. *This Marvellous Woman: A Lesson for
      our Own Times.* Birchington, Kent: Mullan Press, n.d.
      (First appeared in *Christian Order,* October, 1974.)

      This short pamphlet, praising Catherine of Siena, draws

parallels between the saint and her English contemporary
mystic, Julian of Norwich.

750.   Denise, Mary.   "*The Orchard of Syon*: An Introduction."
        Traditio, 14 (1958), 269-93.

A discussion of this work as an important example of
the emerging prose of the 15th century, and as a mystical work which treats of the whole spiritual life of
man, and which is Thomistic, reflecting Catherine's
close association with the Dominicans.   The various
manuscripts are described and compared, together with a
consideration of the Wynkyn de Worde 1519 edition.

751.   Finnegan, Jeremy.   "Catherine in England: *The Orchard
        of Syon*."   *Spirituality Today*, 32 (1980), 13-24.

A discussion of the 15th-century translation of St.
Catherine of Siena's *Dialogue*, accomplished for the
Bridgettine nuns at Syon Abbey.   Finnegan explores
three interlocking themes of the work: God's love for
each person, which encompasses the Motherhood of God
metaphor found in Anselm, the *Ancrene Riwle*, Mechthild
of Hackeborn, and Julian of Norwich; love and service
of one's neighbor and the aspect of human interdependence;
and union of the soul with God.

752.   Foster, Kenelm.   "St. Catherine's Teaching on Christ."
        LS, 16 (1962), 310-23.

An incisive assessment of Catherine's theology and
mysticism as found in the *Dialogue*.

753.   Hodgson, Phyllis.   "*The Orcherd of Syon* and the English
        Mystical Tradition."   Sir Israel Gollancz Memorial
        Lecture.   *Proceedings of the British Academy*, 50
        (1964), 229-49.

Extolling the merits of the *Orcherd* for its content
and its enrichment of the English mystical tradition,
Hodgson explores the manuscript tradition, translation
process, transmission to England, possibly via Dominican
channels, and particular suitability for the Syon nuns.
Moreover, she finds the work reflecting the new interest
in Continental mysticism and women mystics in particular.
Hodgson concludes with a comparison of the *Orcherd* with
the writings of Hilton and Julian of Norwich.

754.   Perrin, J.M.   *Catherine of Siena*.   Trans. Paul Barrett.
        Westminster, Md.: The Newman Press, 1965.

A study of St. Catherine's life, personality, and milieu as revealed in her writings, especially the *Dialogue.*

755. Blessed Raymond of Capua. *The Life of St. Catherine.* Trans. George Lamb. New York: P.J. Kenedy, 1960.

St. Catherine's biography, written by her spiritual director and friend, Raymond of Capua, in support of her canonization.

Remedies Against Temptations, taken from William Flete's *De Remediis Contra Temptaciones*

756. *The remedy ayenst the troubles of temptacyon.* London: Wynkyn de Worde, 1508 (STC 21262); 1519 (STC 20876).

Early editions, erroneously attributed to Richard Rolle.

757. Chadwick, Noel. "The English Version of *De Remediis Contra Temptaciones.*" Diss. Univ. of Liverpool 1963.

758. Colledge, Edmund, and Noel Chadwick. "*Remedies Against Temptations*: The Third English Version of William Flete." *AISP,* 5 (1958), 199-240.

A discussion of the manuscript tradition of the work, annotated descriptions of the various codices, along with Augustine Baker's transcripts, and a critical edition of the third English version.

759. Kirchberger, Clare. "*Strength Against Temptation,* Being an Extract from *De Remediis Contra Tentationes* by William Flete, Transcribed by Walter Hilton." *LS,* 5 (1950), 20-6, 120-5.

A modernized version of the English translation of Flete's treatise, contained in MS. Bodl. 131, which Kirchberger ascribes to Walter Hilton, owing to its similarity with Hilton's translation of the *Stimulus Amoris* into the English *Goad of Love.*

760. Hackett, Benedict. "William Flete and Catherine of Siena." Diss. National Univ. of Ireland 1955.

A detailed account of the life of the English Augustinian William Flete, his seeking the solitary life in Italy, and his close association with St. Catherine of Siena.

761.   ———. "The Spiritual Life of the English Austin
        Friars of the Fourteenth Century." *Sanctus Augustinus
        Vitae Spiritualis Magister*, 2 (1959), 482-92.

        Gives the context and content of three letters from
        William Flete in Italy to his English Augustinian con-
        freres.

762.   ———. "William Flete." *Month*, N.S. 26 (1961), 68-80.

        An analysis of Flete's extant letters and the content
        of the *De Remediis*.

763.   ———. "William Flete and the *De Remediis Contra
        Temptaciones*." In *Medieval Studies Presented to
        Aubrey Gwynn, S.J.* Eds. J.A. Watt, J.B. Morrall,
        and F.X. Martin. Dublin: Three Candles, 1961, pp.
        330-48.

        A discussion of the Latin and English manuscripts of
        the *De Remediis*.

764.   ———, E. Colledge, and Noel Chadwick. "William Flete's
        De Remediis Contra Temptaciones in its Latin and
        English Recensions: The Growth of a Text." *MS*, 26
        (1964), 210-30.

        An examination of the Latin and Middle English manu-
        scripts of the *De Remediis* to assign sources (which
        include the *Ancrene Riwle* and *Stimulus Amoris*); to dis-
        prove that Hilton translated the work, based on a com-
        parison with his translation of the *Stimulus Amoris*;
        to study textual expansions in the three English trans-
        lations; and to illustrate how the Middle English version
        came to be falsely ascribed to Rolle. All versions re-
        tain Flete's primary purpose of bringing consolation
        and counsel to the distressed soul.

The Revelations of St. Birgitta of Sweden, taken from
    her *Liber Celestis*

765.   *Revelationes Sanctae Birgittae*. Imp. B. Ghotan. Lübeck,
        1492.

        The standard edition of the whole work. (Note: A
        critical edition of the Latin text is being undertaken
        in the series *Samlingar utg. av Svenska fornskriftsälls-
        kapet* [*SFSS*], Ser. II [Latinska Skrifter].)

765a. Cumming, William P., ed. *The Revelations of Saint
      Birgitta*. EETS O.S. 178. London: Oxford Univ. Press,
      1929.

      Selections from a 15th-century manuscript in the
      Garrett Collection at Princeton University Library,
      with introduction and notes.

766. Graf, Ernest, trans. *Revelations and Prayers of St.
      Bridget of Sweden*. New York: Benziger Bros., 1928.

      Selections from the *Sermo Angelicus* of St. Bridget
      in a translation undertaken for the Sisters of Syon
      Abbey, South Brent.

767. Butkovich, Anthony. *Revelations: St. Birgitta of Sweden*.
      Los Angeles: Ecumenical Foundation of America, 1972.

      An encomium to St. Bridget, with an account of her
      life, times, and ongoing influence. This is the third
      book of a trilogy: *Anima Eroica*, 1968, and *Iconography
      of St. Birgitta*.

The Seven Points of True Love and Everlasting Wisdom,
  from Henry Suso's *Orologium Sapientiae* (*Büchlein der
  ewigen Weisheit*)

768. Horstmann, Carl. *Orologium Sapientiae or The Seven
      Poynts of Trewe Wisdom Aus MS. Douce 114.*" *Anglia*,
      10 (1888), 323-89.

      A brief introduction and the Middle English version
      of Suso's *Orologium Sapientiae*, which is the Latin
      translation of his *Büchlein der ewigen Weisheit*.

769. Clark, James M., ed. *Little Book of Eternal Wisdom and
      Little Book of Truth by Henry Suso*. London: Faber
      and Faber, Ltd., 1953.

      Clark's introduction discusses the precedence of the
      Büchlein der ewigen Weisheit over the Latin *Orologium
      Sapientiae*, and presents a full analysis of the *Little
      Book of Truth* and of Suso's mystical sources and
      teachings. His English translation is based on Karl
      Bihlmeyer's critical edition.

770. Colledge, E. "The *Büchlein der ewigen Weisheit* and the
      Horologium Sapientiae." *Dominican Studies*, 6 (1953),
      77-89.

      A careful analysis and comparison of the two texts

and a rather negative assessment of J.M. Clark's work
on Suso, and of Clark's contention that the *Horologium*
was only a Latin version of the *Büchlein*.

771. Schleich, G. "Zur Textgestaltung der mittelenglischen
Bearbeitung von Suso's *Orologium Sapientiae*." *Archiv*,
152 (1927), 36-50, 178-92.

A close comparison of the Middle English translation,
Sevene Poyntes of Trewe Loue and Everlastynge Wisdome,
edited by Horstmann (see 768), with the Latin *Orologium*,
edited by Joseph Strange, which sheds light on the
Middle English translation process.

772. ———. "Über die Enstehungzeit und den Verfasser der
mittelenglischen Bearbeitung von Suso's *Horologium*."
Archiv, 157 (1930), 26-34.

A comparative study of pertinent sections of Suso's
Horologium, the Middle English *Sevene Poyntes*, Nicholas
Love's Middle English translation of the *Mirror of the
Blessed Life of Jesus Christ*, and Hilton's *Scale of
Perfection*. Schleich concludes that the *Sevene Poyntes*
was translated during Richard II's reign, and that
Hilton was not its translator.

773. Wichgraf, Wiltrud. "Suso's *Horologium Sapientiae* in
England nach Handschriften des 15. Jahrhunderts."
Anglia, 53 (1929), 123-33, 269-87, 345-73; and 55
(1931), 351-2.

A four-part study on the manuscript tradition and the
work.

774. ———. "Suso's *Horologium Sapientiae* in England nach
MSS. des 15. Jahrhunderts." *Archiv*, 169 (1936), 176-
81.

A descriptive study of six more 15th-century manuscripts of the *Sevene Poyntes*. (See 802-3.)

The Twelve Profits of Tribulation (H 2, 45-60, 391-406),
from the *Duodecim Utilitates Tribulationis*, attributed
to Peter of Blois

775. Kreuzer, James E. "*The Twelve Profits of Anger*." *PMLA*,
53 (1938), 78-85.

A metrical version of *The Twelve Profits of Tribulation*,
with "anger" used in its original significance, i.e.,

tribulation, affliction. It is preserved in two 15th-
century manuscripts: Cambridge Univ. Ff.2.38 and
Pepys 1584. There is no direct relationship between
the Middle English prose and metrical versions, both
descending from a Latin original. The text of the poem
is provided. (Note: A comparison of the metrical and
prose versions clearly illustrates N.F. Blake's finding
regarding the excision of mystical elements from versi-
fied versions of prose texts, so as to appeal to a more
general audience [see 202].)

C. COMPILATIONS

Compilations incorporate a large amount of
didactic, devotional, and mystical material,
all directed toward the achievement of the
perfect spiritual life, inasmuch as it can
be achieved on this earth.

Disce Mori

776. *Disce Vivere: Learne to Live, Disce Mori: Learne to Die.*
London: I. Beale and T. Brundell for N. Bourne, 1629.

There are numerous early editions of the *Disce Mori*,
ranging from 1600 to 1662 (STC 2374-81, Wing 56207) and
in the 19th century.

777. Chadwick, Noel. "An Edition of the *Disce Mori*, Introduction and Seven Deadly Sins." M.A. Thesis Liverpool Univ. 1966.

778. Comper, Frances M.M., ed. *The Book of the Craft of
Dying and Other Early English Tracts Concerning
Death.* London, 1917.

779. Hodgson, Phyllis. "*Ignorancia Sacerdotum*: A Fifteenth
Century Discourse on the Lambeth Constitutions."
RES, 24 (1948), 1-11.

This article discusses the content and style of the
Ignorancia Sacerdotum, a priest's manual, and argues
for increased scholarly attention to the large body of
Middle English works of doctrinal and moral instruction
which evince medieval thought and, often, felicitous
Middle English expression.

780. Hudson, Anne. "A Chapter from Walter Hilton in Two
      Middle English Compilations." *Neophilologus*, 52
      (1968), 16-21.

      Discusses inclusion of Rolle, Hilton, and the *Miroir
      du Monde* in two compilations, the *Disce Mori* and its
      derivative *Ignorancia Sacerdotum*, the latter also con-
      taining extracts from *The Chastising of God's Children*.
      Hudson cites how these compilations "provide interesting
      instances of the multiplication of works of a didactic
      and devotional kind, which might within them increase
      the circulation of certain parts of the writings of the
      great English mystics."

781. Russell, G.H. "Vernacular Instruction of the Laity in
      the Later Middle Ages in England." *Journal of
      Religious History*, 2 (1962), 98-119.

      An assessment of selected Latin and Middle English
      catechetical writings of the 13th, 14th, and 15th
      centuries in England, produced as a result of the
      Fourth Lateran Council (1215) and subsequent English
      councils, notably Pecham's *Ignorancia Sacerdotum*.

Of Actyf Lyfe and Contemplatyf Declaracion and
  Via ad Contemplacionem

782. Jolliffe, Peter. "Two Middle English Tracts on the
      Contemplative Life." *MS*, 37 (1975), 85-121.

      Presents texts and comments on the above works, con-
      tained in two 15th-century manuscripts of Carthusian
      provenance: MSS. B.L. Add. 37790 and 37049. Both tracts
      show borrowings from the *Cloud*, Hilton's *Scale*, Rolle's
      Form of Living, and Hugh of Balma's *Mystica Theologica*.

Of the Knowledge of Ourselves and of God

783. Walsh, James, and E. Colledge. "*Of the Knowledge of
      Ourselves and of God*: A Fifteenth Century Spiritual
      Florilegium." *Month*, 24 (1960), 865-76.

      A study of a pre-Reformation manuscript at Westminster
      Cathedral, which was identified in 1955 as a florilegium
      on the contemplative life, written by one scribe, and
      incorporating the *Commentary* on Pss. 90 and 91 (see
      465), selections from the *Scale*, and Julian's *Revelations*.
      See the Modern English text in the authors' book of the
      same title, published at London: Mowbray & Co., Ltd.,
      1961.

The Poor Caitiff

784. Brady, Mary Teresa. *"The Pore Caitif.* Edited from MS.
      B.L. Harley 2336, with Introduction and Notes." Diss.
      Fordham Univ. 1954.

785. ————. *"The Pore Caitif*: An Introductory Study."
      Traditio, 10 (1954), 529-48.

      Sees *The Pore Caitif* as a religious handbook for the
      home, not original but a compilation, and discusses
      the nature and contents of the work, along with the
      problem of its Lollard associations. Through manuscript
      comparisons, Brady establishes the authentic contents
      and order of the work, and finds no internal traces of
      Lollardry.

786. ————. "The Apostles and the Creed in Manuscripts of
      The Pore Caitif." *Speculum*, 32 (1957), 323-5.

      In eight manuscripts of *The Pore Caitif*, the exposition
      of the Creed rejects the legend which attributes each
      section of the Creed to a specific apostle, an omission
      which may be the result of Lollard interpolation.

787. Sargent, Michael G. "A Source of the *Poor Caitiff*
      Tract 'Of Man's Will.'" *MS*, 41 (1979), 535-9.

      Sargent illustrates that a large part of the contem-
      plative part of the *Poor Caitiff* came from the *Emendatio
      Vitae* of Richard Rolle, and the "Quandoque tribularis
      del temptaris" and "Oleum effusum" compilations.

Speculum Spiritualium

788. *Speculum Spiritualium.* Paris, 1510.

      (Note: This edition was published by Wolfgang Hopyl,
      at the expense of William Bretton, a citizen of London,
      for sale at St. Paul's. The work is a 15th-century
      Latin compilation by an anonymous author [possibly
      Carthusian], presenting, according to Horstmann [H 1,
      p. vii, n. 1], "a complete theory of contemplation,"
      through selections from Bernard, Hilton, and Rolle,
      among others. One of the Rolle extracts from the *Form
      of Living* is given in English, because the compiler
      felt it sounded better in Rolle's English than in
      Latin.)

789. Allen, Hope Emily. "Two Middle English Translations
      from the Anglo-Norman." *MP*, 13 (1916), 741-5.

      Refutes Richard Methley's conjectured authorship of
      the *Speculum Spiritualium*.

The Treatise of Love

790. Fisher, John H., ed. *The Tretyse of Loue*. EETS O.S.
      223. London: Oxford Univ. Press, 1951 (for 1945);
      rpt. 1970.

      A critical edition of this compilation of ten tracts.
      The most mystical part is *The Branches of the Apple
      Tree* (pp. 108-18), which concerns the tree of contempla-
      tion, and partakes in the *Psalma Contemplationis* tradi-
      tion.

791. Hamelin, Marie. "The Middle English Devotional Pieces:
      Þe *Passioun of Oure Lord* and Þe *Treatys of Love*:
      Edition and Commentary." Diss. Fordham Univ. 1962.

      Hamelin finds that the *Treatise*, which concerns Divine
      Love, belongs to the affective school of devotional
      writing, and shows the influence of earlier mystical
      writers, especially Bernard of Clairvaux. The work
      develops a courtly love aura from terms used and atti-
      tudes assumed, which distinguishes it from Rolle's
      writings.

VIII. THE ONGOING TRADITION

The Reformation did not completely stifle
the message of the medieval English mystics, for their works continued to be read
and circulated in England. Moreover, the
exiled Recusant communities on the Continent, especially at Cambrai, Douai, and
Paris, not only preserved the spiritual
writings of the English mystics, but also
authored new mystical texts. Other post-
Reformation mystical texts were authored
by Giles Brewse, Richard Whytford, and
Benet of Canfield (William Fitch).

This section of the bibliography is
organized as follows:
A. The Post-Reformation Period in England.
B. The Recusants on the Continent: The
   Cambrai Community; Fr. Augustine Baker;
   Fr. Serenus Cressy; and Dame Gertrude
   More.
C. Three English Mystics of the Post-
   Reformation Period.
D. Summary.

Note: In both B and C, editions of the
works precede critical articles.

A. THE POST-REFORMATION PERIOD IN ENGLAND

792. Campbell, W.E. "Sermons and Religious Treatises." In
     The Thought and Culture of the English Renaissance.
     Ed. Elizabeth Nugent. Cambridge: Cambridge Univ.
     Press, 1956, pp. 388-93.

     Concerns the continuing impact of medieval traditions
     on Tudor works.

793. Collins, Joseph B. *Christian Mysticism in the Elizabethan
     Age*. Baltimore, Md.: Johns Hopkins Univ. Press, 1940;

rpt. New York: Octagon Books (Farrar, Straus &
Giroux, Inc.), 1971.

While assessing the impact and prevalence of Christian
mysticism in the Elizabethan Age, Collins also presents
a background study in mystical methodology, from its
beginnings in Plato through the patristic period, to its
"golden age" in the late medieval period. Considers
Christian mysticism more from a literary than a theological standpoint.

794.   du Moustier, Benôit.   "English Mysticism in the Life of
       St. Thomas More."   *Spiritual Life*, 5 (1959), 36-42.

       An exploration of the influence of the English mystics
       and the Carthusians on More.

794a. Jones, Judith P.   "'Thy Grace to Set the World at
       Nought': The Mystical Element in the Works of Thomas
       More."   *Studia Mystica*, 2 (1980), 61-71.

       A study of the impact of Christian mysticism on
       More's work and thought.

795.   Kirchberger, Clare.   "Bodleian Manuscripts Relating to
       the Spiritual Life."   *Bodleian Quarterly Record*, 3
       (1951), 155-64.

       An examination of 16th-, 17th-, and 18th-century Bod-
       leian manuscripts dealing with the spiritual life, in-
       cluding works of Hilton, the *Cloud* author, Augustine
       Baker, and Dame Gertrude More.

796.   Lawler, T.M.C.   "Some Parallels Between Walter Hilton's
       Scale of Perfection and St. John Fisher's *Penitential
       Psalms*."   *Moreana*, 9 (1966), 13-27.

       Finds in both works a blend of "practical counsel and
       restrained mysticism," illustrating this thesis with
       parallel passages.

797.   Roberts, John R.   "A Critical Anthology of English Re-
       cusant Prose, 1558-1603."   Diss. Univ. of Illinois
       1962.

       A sampling of English Recusant devotional prose
       written during the reign of Elizabeth.

798.   White, Helen C.   *English Devotional Literature (Prose)
       1600-1640*.   Univ. of Wisconsin Studies in Language and
       Literature 29.   Madison: Univ. of Wisconsin Press, 1931.

A survey of post-Reformation and Counter-Reformation spiritual writing.

799.   ————.   "Some Continuing Traditions in English Devotional Literature." *PMLA*, 57 (1942), 966-80.

An excellent article showing the impact of the Reformation on the medieval works of contemplation, which lost favor, in part, because of their Roman Catholic provenance, or were adapted to reflect the Protestant ethos. White notes that such works as those of Rolle and Hilton continued to be published on Recusant presses, and flourished on the Continent.

800.   ————.   *Tudor Books of Private Devotion.*   Madison: Univ. of Wisconsin Press, 1951.

A survey of the continuum of medieval devotional books, e.g., the Bridgettine *Fifteen Oes*, in the Renaissance.

801.   Wilson, D.D.   "John Wesley and Mystical Prayer."   *LQHR*, 193 (1968), 61-9.

An examination of Wesley's indebtedness to or agreement with the medieval and Counter-Reformation mystics, especially Teresa of Avila, on vocal and silent prayer.

B. THE RECUSANTS ON THE CONTINENT:
THE CAMBRAI COMMUNITY: FR. AUGUSTINE BAKER;
FR. SERENUS CRESSY: DAME GERTRUDE MORE

After the Dissolution, the expulsion of religious orders from England, and their exodus to the Continent, the Carthusians at Sheen Anglorum and the Benedictine convents at Cambrai and Paris became centers for the copying, editing, publishing, and distributing of English mystical texts. The Benedictines Father Augustine Baker and Father Serenus Cressy were also actively involved in writing their own works. Baker's *Sancta Sophia*, as edited by Cressy, is regarded as a spiritual classic. Similarly, Dame Gertrude More, the great-great-granddaughter of the saint, not only fostered the production and preservation of English mystical works at Cambrai, but wrote her own *Spiritual Exercises*.

> Through the efforts of the Recusant religious,
> both the texts and the native English spiri-
> tuality of the medieval mystics were preserved.
> In recent years there has been a revival of
> interest in the Recusants and their leaders,
> which we hope will lead to further substantial
> research and critical editions of such works
> as Father Baker's *Sancta Sophia*.

The Cambrai Community

802.   Rogers, David. "*The Boke of Divers Ghostly Maters*."
       DR, 56 (1938), 427-30.

       A bibliographic note on the history of this text,
       which belonged to Cambrai prior to 1635, and then
       passed to the Paris daughter-house. Considered to be
       the last book printed by Caxton in 1491, it contains
       the *Horologium Sapientiae* (see 768-74), the *Twelve
       Profits of Tribulation* (see 775), and the *Rule of St.
       Benedict*.

803.   ————. "Some Early Devotional Books from Cambrai."
       DR, 57 (1939), 458-63.

       Discusses MS. Cambrai Lib. 1115, which contains tran-
       scripts of three printed opuscules of Richard Whytford,
       and MS. 255, containing the English translation of
       Suso's *Orologium*, which, given the Mount Grace provenance
       of the manuscript, may have been translated by Nicholas
       Love.

804.   Spearritt, Placid. "The Survival of Mediaeval Spiri-
       tuality Among the Exiled Black Monks." *ABR*, 25
       (1974), 287-309.

       A balanced study of the spiritual and liturgical
       activities at Cambrai, involving Augustine Baker,
       Serenus Cressy, and Dames Gertrude More, Catherine
       Gascoigne, and Barbara Constable, with an assessment of
       the current state of Baker studies, an excellent bibliog-
       raphy, and a list of extant Baker manuscripts. Spearritt
       stresses how the efforts of these Benedictines insured
       that the spiritual classics written during the 13th
       and 14th centuries in England were kept in circulation
       after the Reformation.

Father Augustine Baker (1575-1641)

805. Baker, Augustine. *Sancta Sophia, or Directions for the
      Prayer of Contemplation. Extracted out of more than
      40 Treatises written by the late Ven. Father F. Augustin
      Baker, a Monke of the English Congregation of the Holy
      Order of S. Benedict; and Methodically digested by the
      R.F. Serenus Cressy of the Same Order and Congregation.*
      2 Vols. Douay: John Patte and Thomas Fievet, 1657.

806. McCann, Justin, ed. *The Confessions of Venerable
      Father Augustine Baker, O.S.B.* London: Burns, Oates
      & Washbourne, 1922.

      A modern edition of Father Baker's spiritual auto-
      biography.

807. ————, ed. *Life of Father Augustine Baker.* By Peter
      Salvin and Serenus Cressy. London: Burns, Oates &
      Washbourne, 1933.

      An edition of Baker biographies by Salvin and Cressy,
      with an appendix of Baker manuscripts and published
      works.

808. ————, and Hugh Connolly, eds. *Memorials of Father
      Augustine Baker and Other Documents Relating to the
      English Benedictines.* Catholic Record Society 33
      (1933).

      Texts of Baker's unfinished autobiography (pp. 3-52)
      and Prichard's *Life of Father Baker*, taken from MS.
      1755 in the Bibliothèque Mazarine (pp. 53-154): Baker's
      Treatise of the English Benedictine Mission (pp. 155-
      89); and a *Descriptive Catalogue of Baker Manuscripts
      in English and Foreign Libraries* (pp. 274-93).

809. Sitwell, Gerard, ed. *Holy Wisdom; or Directions for
      the Prayer of Contemplation.* London: Burns & Oates,
      1964.

      A new edition, which omits the preface and appendices
      of the 1657 text.

810. Sweeny, J. Norbert, ed. *Holy Wisdom.* London: Burns,
      Oates & Washbourne, 1876; rpt. New York: Harper, 1950.

      A frequently reprinted modern text of the Cressy
      edition.

811.   Weld-Blundell, Benedict, ed. *Prayers and Holiness.*
       *The Teaching of Ven. Augustine Baker Thereon, Taken
       from Sancta Sophia.* London: Magnani, 1933.

812.   Alcott, Edward B. "A Comparison of the Mystical
       Teachings of Walter Hilton and Augustine Baker."
       Diss. St. Louis Univ. 1973.

       Compares three aspects of the pre- and post-Reforma-
       tion Catholic mystics: the teachings on the goal of the
       mystical life; ideas on the necessity of mystical suf-
       ferings, called purgations; and the mystic unitive
       experience itself. Alcott finds that Hilton and Baker
       are in essential agreement, and concludes that tradi-
       tional monastic contemplative ideals did not change
       fundamentally in England due to the Reformation.

813.   Butler, Cuthbert. "Fr. Augustine Baker." *DR*, 51
       N.S. 32 (1933), 377-95.

       A study of Fr. Baker's life; his controversial teach-
       ing, especially on affective prayer and God as the in-
       terior guide of contemplative souls; his difficulties
       with Fr. Barlow; his return to the English Mission;
       and an account of Baker's leading Cambrai disciple, Dame
       Gertrude More.

814.   Cowley, Patrick. "Father Augustine Baker and the Sources
       of the *Sancta Sophia.*" *Theology*, 37 (1938), 6-16.

815.   Hedley, John C. "Father Baker's *Sancta Sophia.*" *Dublin
       Review*, 79 (1876), 337-67. (Also appeared in his
       Evolution and Faith, London: Sheed and Ward, 1931,
       pp. 163-206.)

       A comprehensive discussion of Baker's contemplative
       practices.

816.   Higgins, M. St. Theresa. "Augustine Baker." Diss.
       Univ. of Wisconsin 1963.

       An investigation of the life and teaching of Augustine
       Baker as seen in *Sancta Sophia*, the *Commentary on the
       Cloud of Unknowing*, the *Confessions*, the *Life of Dame
       Gertrude More*, and his partial autobiography. Higgins
       finds his religious writings to be valuable evidence
       in the history of religious thought and the development
       of the English mystical tradition.

817. Low, Anthony. *Augustine Baker.* New York: Twayne Pub-
     lishers, Inc., 1970.

     An extensive biography of Father Baker, along with a
     broad general survey of his works, and a strong *apologia*
     for his important place among the English mystics.
     There is also an excellent annotated bibliography of
     leading studies on Baker.

818. Lunn, D. "Augustine Baker (1575-1641) and the English
     Mystical Tradition." *JEH*, 26 (1975), 267-77.

     A careful exploration of the circumstances of *Sancta
     Sophia*'s publication and a comparative study of Serenus
     Cressy's work with Baker manuscripts, thereby revealing
     the effect of Cressy's editing on Baker's thought and
     teachings.

819. McCann, Justin. "Father Baker's Devotions." *Ampleforth
     Journal*, 34 (1929), 135-50.

820. ————. "Bakerism at Douay Seminary." *CR*, 2 (1931),
     213-26.

     Concerning Fr. Baker's spiritual influence at Douay.

821. ————. "Father Baker's Tercentenary." *DR*, 59 (1941),
     355-71.

     An explanation of why none of Fr. Baker's treatises
     have been published, owing to their form, style, and
     prolixity, and an examination of the relation of *Sancta
     Sophia*, as edited by Serenus Cressy in 1657, to the
     original treatises.

822. ————. "Ten More Baker Manuscripts." *Ampleforth
     Journal*, 63 (1958), 77-83.

     An addendum to Father McCann's continuing search for
     Baker manuscripts.

823. Meredith, Francis. "Forgotten Quatercentenary." *Mount
     Carmel*, 24 (1976), 210-26.

     An encomium to Father Baker, with important bio-
     graphical information.

824. Owen, H.W. "Another Augustine Baker Manuscript." In
     Dr. L. Reypens-Album. Ed. Albert Ampe. Antwerp:

Uitgave Van Het Ruusbroec-Genootschap, 1964, pp. 269-80.

A report on the Upholland anthology, a 17th-century manuscript located at St. Joseph's College, Upholland, Lancashire, its Cambrai provenance, and contents, which include extracts from Julian of Norwich's *Revelations*, possibly ascribable to Father Baker.

825. Watkin, E.I. "A Note on Contemplation." *DR*, N.S. 41 (1942), 299-308.

Attempts to clarify Father Baker's teaching on contemplation, presenting a clear discussion of roles of volition, faith, understanding, and negative knowledge in mystic union, with specific reference to the *Cloud*.

826. ————. "Mysticism." *Spiritual Life*, 5 (1959), 6-21.

An analytical discourse on the mystical life, drawing on Augustine Baker and Abbot Chapman.

Father Serenus Cressy (1605-74)

827. Steuart, Hilary. "A Study in Recusant Prose: Dom Serenus Cressy, 1605-74." *DR*, 66 (1948), 165-78, 287-301.

A survey of the prose writings of Cressy, other than his edition of *Sancta Sophia*. Cites Cressy's edition of Julian's *Revelations* and the popularity of 14th-century mystical works among the devout of the 17th century.

Dame Gertrude More (1606-33)

828. Gascoigne, Francis, ed. *The Spiritual Exercises of the Most Vertuous and Religious D. Gertrude More.* Paris: L. de la Fosse, 1658.

829. Weld-Blundell, Benedict, ed. *The Inner Life and the Writings of Dame Gertrude More.* 2 vols. London: R. & T. Washbourne, 1910-11.

A Modern English version of Dame Gertrude More's *Confessio Amantis* or *The Confessions of a Loving Soul*, and her *Apology* for herself and her spiritual director, Fr. Augustine Baker.

830. Deace, Alice. "Dame Gertrude More." *Ave Maria*, 42 (1935), 138-41.

A study of Gertrude More's life, religious vocation, and spiritual progress under Fr. Augustine Baker's guidance.

831. McCann, Justin. "Father Baker's Dame Gertrude." *DR*, 47 (1929), 157-67.

An early review of some of the manuscript sources of the life of Dame Gertrude, with attention paid to the part played by the material supplied by Father · Baker.

832. Norman, Marion. "Dame Gertrude More and the English Mystical Tradition." *Recusant History*, 13 (1976), 196-211.

Norman takes the position that in richness and variety the literature of mysticism in the early post-Reformation period not only emulates that of the 14th century, but also constitutes a major contribution to the cultural history of the West. The work of the Recusant writers of the second half of the 17th century is virtually an untapped body of material to be explored, Norman affirms. He also points to the influence of the English mystical heritage on the exiled contemplatives, evinced from surviving catalogues of the Sheen Anglorum Charterhouse and the Benedictine libraries at Paris and Cambrai. Norman concludes his essay with an account of the life of Dame Gertrude More.

C. THREE ENGLISH MYSTICS
OF THE POST-REFORMATION PERIOD

Giles Brewse

833. Kirchberger, Clare. "*The Homely Presence of Christ* by Giles Brewse." *LS*, 4 (1949), 109-14.

An edition of Brewse's mystical treatise from MS. Laud. Misc. 19 of the early 16th century, which, according to Kirchberger, links the 14th-century English mystics and especially Walter Hilton, with Reformation spirituality.

Richard Whytford

834. Whytford, Richard. *The Pype/ or Tonne/ of the Lyfe of Perfection*. London: Robert Redman, 1532.

   (Note: Bliss's edition of Wood's *Athenae Oxoniensis* also lists Whytford's translations of the *Rule of St. Augustine* and the *Imitation of Christ*, and contains an interesting section on Whytford as translator on pp. xxiii-v.)

Benet of Canfield (William Fitch)

835. de Vegel, Optat. *Benoit de Canfield (1562-1610): Sa Vie, Sa Doctrine et Son Influence*. Rome, 1949.

   This is an investigation of Benet's life, largely spent in exile in France, his teaching on the contemplative life, stressing conformity to the will of God, and the sources and importance of Benet's *Rule of Perfection*.

836. Emery, Kent. "Translating the Mystics." *Triumph*, 9 (1974), 16-19, 43.

   Contends that in Christian tradition, the way of contemplation should not exclude the layman, supporting this view with texts from the *Cloud* and Benet of Canfield.

837. ————. "'All and Nothing': Benet of Canfield's *Règle de Perfection*." *DR*, 92 (1974), 46-61.

   This essay studies the *Epistle of Privy Counsel*, ascribed to the *Cloud* author, as a source for Benet of Canfield's use of the paradox which was central to his thought--the relation between the all of the Creator and the nothing of the creature.

838. ————. "Benet of Canfield: Counter-Reformation Spirituality and its Medieval Origins." Diss. Univ. of Toronto 1976.

   Benet of Canfield is presented as one of the most significant English Catholic spiritual writers after the Middle Ages, and, in his life, teaching, and *Rule of Perfection*, a continuator of the tradition of medieval English spirituality. This is an important study of a long-neglected mystic.

838a. Gullick, Etta. "Benet of Canfield. *The Rule of Perfection*: The Active and Contemplative Life." *Laurentianum*, 4 (1972), 401-36.

A discussion of the textual tradition and content of the *Rule*.

839. Sheppard, Lancelot C. "Benet of Canfield and his *Rule of Perfection*." *DR*, 69 (1951), 323-32.

A summary of Fr. Optat de Vegel's *Benoit de Canfield*.

840. Sitwell, Gerard. "Benet Canfield." *Month*, N.S. 21 (1959), 218-29.

A treatment of Benet of Canfield as an "eminent exponent of the tradition of contemplative life," a tradition shared by the 14th-century mystics in England, the Rhineland, and the Low Countries, and a careful analysis of his teaching, as presented in the *Rule of Perfection*. Sitwell defends Benet against the charge of Quietism, but criticizes him for "pushing the Dionysian tradition too far and adopting too narrow a concept of it."

D. SUMMARY

841. Birrell, T.A. "English Catholic Mystics in Non-Catholic Circles." *DR*, 94 (1976), 60-81, 99-117, 213-231.

This seminal study presents much precise information about owners of libraries on mysticism and about literary figures who were interested in the English mystics, defended or opposed their teachings, possessed or copied their writings, or wrote works similar in spirit and purpose. Beginning with the above-mentioned Recusants, Birrell traces a continuous tradition in English and American literature of knowledge of the medieval mystics and of their effect on the history of ideas, down to the present day. Birrell states that a full-scale history of English mysticism has yet to be written, and should encompass a history of this authentic Western mystical tradition as an integral part of our total culture. He also feels that accounts of the English mystics should be incorporated into literary history as it is now taught. Although Birrell modestly calls his essays "a catena of facts," they represent an important contribution to literary history and a challenge to further research.

APPENDIX:
FORTHCOMING EDITIONS AND STUDIES

Abbey of the Holy Ghost. Ed. Peter Consacro. Scheduled for
EETS.

Benet of Canfield. *The Rule of Perfection*. Ed. Kent Emery.
Classics of Western Spirituality, Paulist Press.

Charter of the Abbey of the Holy Ghost. Ed. Elizabeth
Fanning. Scheduled for EETS.

Classics of Western Spirituality, Paulist Press. An ongoing
series of modern translations of Western spiritual writings.

Hilton, Walter. A critical edition of *The Scale of Perfection*.
Eds. A.J. Bliss and Stanley S. Hussey. Scheduled for
EETS.

Hogg, James, ed. *Mount Grace Charterhouse and Late Medieval
English Spirituality*. Analecta Cartusiana 64. Salzburg,
1981-2. To include the Latin works of John Norton and
Richard Methley.

Index of Middle English Prose in Print, 1476-1976. Eds. N.F.
Blake, A.S.G. Edwards, and Robert E. Lewis. Garland
Publishing, Inc. This is the first stage of the *Index
of Middle English Prose*, which, when completed, will
encompass a first-line index of all Middle English prose
texts. Also published by Garland Publishing, Inc., is
Middle English Prose: Essays in Bibliographical Problems,
ed. A.S.G. Edwards and Derek Pearsall, 1981, containing
the proceedings of the *IMEP* Conference at Emmanuel College,
Cambridge, in July, 1978.

Kennedy, David G. *The Incarnational Element in Hilton's
Spirituality*. Elizabethan and Renaissance Studies 96.
Salzburg, 1981.

Pelphrey, Brant. *Love Was His Meaning: The Mystical Theology
of Julian of Norwich*. Elizabethan and Renaissance
Studies 92. Salzburg, 1981.

*The Rewyll of Seynt Sauioure Vol. 3: The Syon Additions for
the Brethren and The Boke of Sygnes from the St. Paul's
Cathedral Library MS. Vol. 4: The Syon Additions for the
Sisters from the British Library MS. Arundel 146.* Ed.
James Hogg. Salzburger Studien zur Anglistik und Amerikan-
istik 8, 1980.

Rich, Edmund. *Merure de Seynte Eglise.* Ed. A.D. Wilshere.
Anglo-Norman Text Society.

Riehle, Wolfgang. *The Middle English Mystics: A Study of
Metaphor and Language.* Routledge and Kegan Paul, 1980.
An English translation of his *Studien zur englischen
Mystik des Mittelalters unter besonderer Berücksichtigung
ihrer Metaphorik.*

Rolle, Richard. *Emendatio Vitae. The Non-Misyn Translations.*
Ed. Margaret Amassian. Middle English Texts, Heidelberg.

————. *The Fire of Love and Amending of Life.* Ed. M.L. del
Mastro. Doubleday & Co., Inc., 1981.

Speculum Inclusorum in MS. B.L. Harl. 2372. A Critical Edition.
Ed. James Hogg. Analecta Cartusiana 59. Salzburg.

Whytford, Richard. *The Pype or Tonne of the Lyfe of Perfec-
tion.* Ed. James Hogg. With an introductory study on
Whytford's works and appendices containing *A Werke for
Householders* and *A Daily Exercyse and Experyence of
Dethe.* Elizabethan and Renaissance Studies 89. Salzburg.

INDEX

A.P., 268

Aarts, Florent G., 326

Abbacio de Sancto Spiritu. See *Abbey of the Holy Ghost*

L'Abbaye du Saint Esprit. See *Abbey of the Holy Ghost*

Abbey of the Holy Ghost, 100, 157, 200, 686-91, 720

Ackerman, R.W., 146

Adler, Max, 327

The Adornment of the Spiritual Marriage (Ruysbroeck), 696

Aelred of Rievaulx, 101, 141, 144-5, 216, 229, 623, 709-11

Ahern, Barnabas, 1

Albert, Sr. Mary, 531-3

Alcott, Edward, 812

Alford, John A., 355-6

Allchin, A.M., 534-6

Allen, Hope Emily, 114, 298-9, 317, 331-2, 357-60, 622, 655, 789

Allen, Sr. M. Edwards, 502

Alphonse of Pecha, 678

Amassian, Margaret, 297, 361

Ancrene Riwle, 114, 128, 146, 152, 161, 205-6, 216, 225, 241, 378, 481, 493, 538, 593, 751, 764

Anhede of Godd with Mannes Soule (*Of Angels' Song*), 325

Annunziata, Anthony, 651

Anselm of Canterbury, 115-6, 123, 124-5, 143, 236, 481, 623, 659, 751

Appulby, Simon, 673

Armstrong, A.H., 117

Arnould, Emile F.J., 250, 333-6

Arntz, Mary L., 328

Ashley, Benedict, 748

Ashley, Kathleen M., 199

Atkinson, Clarissa, 623

Attwater, Donald, 3

Augustine of Hippo, 8, 135, 463, 492, 542, 589

Baker, Albert E., 537

Baker, Augustin, 84, 153, 168, 173, 183, 196, 389, 433, 453, 490, 758, 795, 804-26

177

Formula Noviciorum, 229, 706, 708
Forshaw, Helen P., 718, 726-7
Foster, Kenelm, 752
Foulds, Elfrida, 561
Fox, George, 150
Francis of Assisi, St., 123, 369
Free Spirit Heresy, 472, 733, 738-41
Frères du Libre Esprit, 84
Friends of God, 11, 39, 62, 557
Froomberg, Hilary, 282, 292

Gardet, Louis, 22
Gardiner, H.C., 92
Gardner, Edmund G., 105
Gardner, Helen L., 408, 480-1
Garrett, Robert M., 686
Garrigou-Lagrange, Reginald, 23-4
Garrison, Anne, 390
Gascoigne, Catherine, 804
Gascoigne, Francis, 828
Gatta, Julie M., 160
Gatto, Louis C., 408a
Gauvin, C., 213
Gehring, Hester McNeal Reed, 214
Gerard of Liège, 229, 703-5
Gerlach, George, 517
Gertrude of Helfta, 212
Gheestelijcke Brulocht. See Spiritual Espousals (Ruysbroeck)
Gibinska, Marta, 304
Gilmour, J., 364
Gish, Nancy K., 215
Glasscoe, Marion, 160a, 513
Glaube und Erfahrung, 462
   See also Scale of Perfection (Hilton)
Goad of Love (Hilton), 447-9, 494, 759, 764
Goulianos, Joan, 635
Goyau, Lucie Felix-Faure, 161
Goymer, C.B., 719
Grady, Sr. Laureen, 391, 421
Graef, Hilda C., 25-7, 518, 562
Graf, Ernest, 766
Gray, Douglas, 305
Green, Carol Hurd, 639
Gregory of Nyssa, 586
Gregory the Great, 8, 475, 492, 727
Groote, Gerard, 702
Guarnieri, Romana, 84, 733, 736-7, 741

Super Psalmum Vicesimum (Rolle), 260
Suso, Henry, 11, 109, 123, 242, 593, 768-74, 802-3
Sweeney, J. Norbert, 810
Sylvia Mary, Sr., 70
Syon Abbey, 167, 676-7, 679-82, 684, 693, 751

Takamiya, Toshiyuki, 442, 497
Talbot, Charles H., 710, 717
A Talking of the Love of God, 224-5, 233-4, 668-71
Tanner, Norman P., 601
Tanquerey, Adolphe, 71
Tart, Charles T., 72
Tauler, 11, 109, 182, 593
Taylor, V., 602
Teilhard de Chardin, 578
Teresa of Avila, St., 495, 577, 801
Theiner, Paul F., 261
Thomas Aquinas, St., 160, 475, 576, 589
Thompson, E. Margaret, 192
Thompson, Meredith, 670
Thornton, Martin, 193, 644
Thorold, Algar, 747
Thouless, Robert Henry, 603
Thurston, Herbert, 645
To Hew Heremyte A Pystyl of Solytary Lyfe Nowadayes, 672
Treatise of Discretion of Spirits. See *Cloud* author
Treatise of Discretion of Stirrings. See *Cloud* author
Treatise of Love, 790-1
Treatise of Perfection of the Sons of God, 694
   See also *The Sparkling Stone* (Ruysbroeck)
Treatise of the English Benedictine Mission (Augustine Baker),
      810
Trethowan, Illtyd, 460
Tretyse of the Stodye of Wysdome That Men Clepen Beniamyn.
      See *Cloud* author
Tuma, George W., 194
Twelve Profits of Anger, 775
Twelve Profits of Tribulation, 775, 802
Tyrrell, George, 525, 604

Ullmann, J., 295
Underhill, Evelyn, 73-4, 269, 351, 385, 403, 461, 463, 465,
      696, 743
Undset, Sigrid, 646

Vaisser, J.J., 656
Van den Blinckenden Steen. See *The Sparkling Stone* (Ruysbroeck)
Vandenbroucke, Francis, 171, 253